Original Sin
Ritual Child Rape & the Church

by Dr. DCA Hillman

RONIN
Berkeley, California

Original Sin
Ritual Child Rape & the Church

by Dr. DCA Hillman

Original Sin

ISBN: 978-1-57951-144-9

Published by

Ronin Publishing, Inc.

PO Box 22900

Oakland, CA 94609

www.roninpub.com

Credits:

Illustrations are from Clipart.com

Cover: Michael Pacher, 'The Devil Showing St. Augustine the Book of Vices,' circa 1480

Production:

Cover & Book Design: Beverly A. Potter.
Editor: Mark J. Estren, Ph.D.

Library of Congress Card Number: 2012948278

Distributed to the book trade by PGW/Perseus

Dedication

FOR LIVIA: Never take your eye off the Muse.

Also by Dr. DCA Hillman

The Chemical Muse

Table of Contents

1 Exclusive Sodomy 9
2 The Way 19
3 Defining Youth 27
4 Feminine Foundations of Civilization 35
5 Paralyzing Child Protection 44
6 Creating Homosexuals and Whores 51
7 Political Power and Pornography 57
8 Religious Hot-Boxing 62
9 Reinforcing Rape with Sobriety 69
10 Shattering an Old Paradigm 75
11 A Monk by Any Other Name 82
12 Redefining Women 89
13 Christianity's Promotion of Pedophilia 97
14 Death of the Muses 103
15 To Think Like a Priest 110
16 Mystery of the Lady-Boy 117
17 What Would Jesus Do with Breasts? 125
18 The Child Rape Ritual Exposed 132
Epilogue 141
Author Bio 145

Dr. Hillman seated in front of an ecstatic follower of Dionysus. This drunken satyr promotes a conception of the gods that provokes a viscerally negative response from Christian culture. This satyr in ecstasy—possibly Dionysus himself—is unlike most ancient sculpture because of the focus on the pubic region as a statement of the power of the mysteries.

Chapter 1

Exclusive Sodomy

The sodomizing of young children by the Christian clergy is a practice as old as the Catholic Church itself. Most people today believe that the gruesome activities of priest pedophiles are an unfortunate reality of a religious hierarchy that promotes celibacy and deters its priests from experiencing any form of sexual pleasure. However, child abuse in the Church is profoundly institutional. From the earliest centuries of Christianity, priests, elders, monks and bishops established, promoted and defended the ritual rape of young boys. Child abuse is not an accident of Church history; it is an integral, foundational component of Christianity.

Ritual child rape performed by Christian priests was very much the result of a cultural war declared by religious zealots during the first few centuries of the Church. The earliest generations that followed the birth and death of Jesus witnessed incredible social upheaval on an unparalleled scale. Europe, North Africa and parts of Asia were all inextricably knotted up in the affairs of the political behemoth called the Roman Empire. The unity that so characterized the Roman world facilitated a head-to-head social conflict of Christians and non-Christians.

The polytheistic core of classical religion effortlessly adapted itself to encounters with new divinities from the East, but the arrival of proselytizing Christian monotheists in the Common Era was the beginning of the end for the Roman way of life. The Roman pantheon of gods, despite its inclusive tendencies, quickly succumbed to the demands of the Christian priestly hierarchy that flourished on the basis of its pronounced exclusivity.

Christian priests did not blend into the classical world. They were known for their uniqueness. Common members of the early Church were secretive and isolated. Monks were lone, intolerant zealots, beyond the reach of custom and law. Priests refused to swear allegiance to the emperor. Common Christians dropped out of society and became highly secretive. Mystery initiations involving the rape of children served to reinforce the Church's efforts to set its members apart from the rest of the general population while rigorously promoting the not-to-be-questioned authority of its clergy.

The non-Christians who lived during the rise of the Christian Church claimed they were witnessing the end of civilization. The Greeks and Romans might have invented democracy, science and medicine, but their shared culture eventually resigned itself to defeat; in the face of the rapidly expanding power of an exclusively male priesthood, known for its novel views of sex, Roman educators, bureaucrats and politicians slowly ceded their cultural traditions to Church dogma.

The foundation of classical religion was its enthusiastic veneration of beauty. Unlike the rest of the classical world, the Christians employed general moral definitions of "good" and "evil" that made their followers unique. The Greeks and Romans believed individual inquiry determined morality. But for Christians living anywhere in the empire, under the auspices of any ethnic group, there was one cultural constant: Jesus was the standard of morality, not Nature. Ignatius, the bishop of Antioch and student of the Apostle John, was among the earliest of Christians to establish the concept of orthodox language, in his *Letter to the Ephesians*. In doing so he helped to limit any form of criticism of Church officials—a concession that non-Christian priests were never granted.

> The Christians would bring us a society without law. They would teach us to have no fear of the gods.
>
> —PORPHYRY ON THE DANGERS OF CHRISTIANITY

The Term "Pagan"

As orthodox speech and doctrine came to the fore of the ancient stage, Christians began calling non-Christians "pagans." It was a pejorative term, like our modern "hillbilly" or "redneck," and the word was meant to describe anyone who refused to follow the Christian messiah as the source of universal truth. Of course it was arrogantly condescending, but it was primarily a means of isolating non-Christians as morally distinct from the growing numbers of Christians.

In the early centuries of the Common Era, monks and priests increasingly painted pagans in a negative moral light based on their age-old use of drugs in religious rituals; the Christians portrayed them as spiritual criminals. Drugs had long been a staple of the back-woodsy, Roman religious cults.

Prominent Church fathers worked diligently to root out the use of drugs in their own meetings and celebrations in order to distinguish themselves from pagan religions steeped in the use of psychotropics. The earliest Christian Eucharist was referred to as the "drug of immortality," but Christian priests worked diligently to distinguish their own drug use from that of non-Christians. In his *Letter to the Ephesians*, Ignatius, who assumed a title commonly reserved for important pagan priests, taught that the use of non-Christian drugs was tantamount to the rejection of orthodoxy: "Therefore I am urging you—not I, but the love of Jesus Christ—make use only of Christian food and abstain from a foreign plant, which is heresy."

By the fourth century, thanks to the power of the bishops, Roman laws were written to ban the use of drugs in any sort of cultic practices—under penalty of execution. This gave the bishops legal authority to arrest drug-using pagans and to seize their property.

Assets from drug seizures were directly absorbedby the Church. The pagans viewed this assimilation of public wealth by the Church as an injustice and evidence of the corrupt motives of Christian priests. Pagans had long sus-

VENUS, CUPID AND MARS, POMPEII.

pected that Christianity was a convenient way to get rich. The pagan philosopher Porphyry, in *Against the Christians*, expressed the common sentiment this way: "The words of Christ, 'I came not to bring peace but a sword. I came to separate a son from his father,' belie the true intentions of the Christians. They seek riches and glory. Far from being friends of the empire, they are renegades waiting for their chance to seize control."

The first western drug war started in earnest in the third and fourth centuries. Bishops and priests were its most prominent backers; as a group, Christian clergy members may have been separated by doctrinal disputes, but they all shared a desire to advance their own political causes. Priests didn't care what Romans and Greeks put in their bodies; they simply wanted to solidify their growing hold on empire. And one of the means of doing so was to assert legal control over the non-Christian population in a way that assured tight social control.

Unable to perform their sacraments legally, the pagans went underground. In the process, members of pagan religions became politically disenfranchised. And for the first time in history, drugs took on a negative moral connotation. Drugs and drug users, like prostitutes and homosexuals, became taboo and illegal.

The use of drugs was not the only physical pleasure made illicit by the early Christians. For the first five centuries of the Common Era, priests, monks, bishops and Church elders consistently labored to make sexual intercourse itself an act of moral contamination. In one of the greatest reversals of human history, the western world turned from embracing sexual intercourse to considering it a form of pollution.

One set of facts was constant in all of the Christian priesthood: there was a patent, open, doctrinal hatred for women, homosexuals and drugs. The cultural war that started in the early centuries of the Common Era, and ultimately produced modernity, was driven by the ideology of these priests. As bishops gained the ear of the imperial bureaucracy, the court, and eventually the emperor himself, they promoted the values of exclusivity that had been so successful in bolstering their own ranks.

Sex Is Not Healthy

According to the apostles and the early Church fathers, sex was not a healthy act that brought new life into the world—as the pagan world saw it—but was the tool of the devil. Sex merely distracted the Christian pilgrim from the path to paradise, and as Paul famously argued, was better avoided.

Church fathers like Tertullian worked incessantly to create an image of sex and sexual attraction as strictly negative phenomena. Despite the fact that bishops were known to keep lovers in the ranks of their "virgins," early Church fathers are unified in their public condemnation of sexual intercourse, as in Tertullian's *On the Veiling of Virgins*.

For the Greco-Roman world, sex was the highest expression of good; it was the ultimate beauty that propelled the natural world forward. Desire was one of the greatest creative forces of the universe. Aphrodite, the goddess of attraction, was worshipped in Greece, and in Egypt, and in Phoenicia and even further east. The same divinity had different names. She was Venus, Astarte, Isis and Ishtar. And her priestesses were known throughout the Mediterranean world. Moreover, her followers honored and worshiped her with the use of drugs. For example, on the island of Cyprus,

> She whom the Africans worship as the Heavenly One, the Persians as Mithra and the multitude as Venus has a variety of names but is not a different divinity.
>
> —AMBROSE
>
> ON THE MANY MANIFESTATIONS OF APHRODITE

MICHELANGELO

Aphrodite's temple burned all-year-round with incense that contained potent psychotropic botanicals. In the pagan mind, these drugs acted as a conduit through which the goddess could possess her mortal followers.

The cult of Aphrodite was allied with the worship of Dionysus, the god of ecstasy. As a matter of fact, one Greek historian, Herodotus, asserted in *The Histories* that even the Arabs worshipped the two gods as their primary deities. Dionysus was the god of wine itself. And wine in antiquity was not just wine; it was a base for mixing alcohol-soluble drugs. Wine was the key ingredient in pharmacological potions that intoxicated religious observers and filled them with visions of the gods.

Like Aphrodite, Dionysus was a mantic god. That meant he had the power of prophecy—the power to explain the past, the present and the future. The lyric poet Anacreon, in his *Fragments*, makes it clear that Dionysus was nothing less than a Muse. And like Aphrodite, Dionysus was worshiped in both the East and the West. Whether he was Osiris of Egypt, Bacchus of Rome, or Zagreus of Thrace, Dionysus was the god of "entheos" or possession. And according to the ancient world, he always led his followers to Aphrodite—to sexual desire.

The followers of Dionysus were almost exclusively women. His priestesses were women. His Maenads ranged across mountains, screaming and dancing in celebration of their god. They were intoxicated, divinely inspired women, who freely consumed the wine of the god and thus became maddened. Their wildly independent activities earned them the special ire of the Christians. The Christian author Firmicus Maternus, in *The Error of the Pagan Religions*, claimed their celebrations brought out the natural corruptive sexual desires of women. He further claimed that the Christian Eucharist was a remedy for the drugs of Dionysus.

> Come, thou frenzy-stricken one, not resting on thy wand, not wreathed with ivy! Cast off thy headdress; cast off thy fawnskin; return to soberness! I will show thee the Word, and the Word's mysteries, describing them according to thine own semblance of them.
>
> —CLEMENT OF ALEXANDRIA
> EXHORTATION TO THE GREEKS

The Maenads who followed Dionysus—and ultimately Aphrodite—celebrated a single individual... someone called the Kore. In the Greek language a "kore" is a post-pubertal girl, someone who has recently developed the ability to create life. In the classical mind, the kore was a mortal who had been freshly initiated into the cyclical rites of Nature. She understood the rhythms of life; she understood the power of creativity, and she understood the sway of madness.

The kore was a young girl—just a teenager—but so were the gods and goddesses of the ancient world. The Greek title "koura" is used to describe many goddesses. Aphrodite was depicted in myth and art as a teenage kore; the Muses were teenagers; the Fates were teenagers. Athena, Persephone and Artemis were all teenage girls. It's fair to say the Greeks and the Romans worshipped youth because it was untouched by age—the mark of mortals. And the beauty—or sexual attraction—of the kore was considered a sign of her eternality.

The first oracles, the most powerful priestesses of the ancient world, were all young girls. For example, the teenage girls who made up the chorus that staged public performances in honor of the cult of Apollo on the island of Delos were among the earliest of oracular priestesses. The author of the archaic hymns attributed to Homer celebrates the uncanny ability of these girls to engage their audiences in the *Hymn to Delian Apollo*. Young priestesses were referred to as "nightingales," and some of the earliest lyric poems were the famous "maiden songs."

The Greeks believed that girls who had recently acquired the ability to produce offspring were closer to the gods than any other living human. They believed these girls were the most divinely inspired; they believed they had the greatest sense of justice. And the Greeks considered these girls to be the most fearless of mortals. In short, the ancient kore earned the right to become the mouthpiece of the cosmos.

As a result of these beliefs, the Greeks created the first western choruses from the ranks of young teenage girls. These ancient choruses composed hymns in praise of their gods, performed public services, and pronounced oracles. They were educated in the arts of dance, poetry, astronomy, geometry and pharmacy. They could alter their own menstrual cycle, paralyze an enemy with snake-venom-tipped arrows, or induce states of inspirational ecstasy. And they performed their dances to packed crowds across the Mediterranean. Their physical beauty was considered a reflection of the divine power of the universe. And as a result, they were hated by the first Christian priests.

The profound cultural sway of the cults of Aphrodite and Dionysus made them a target for the priests and bishops of Christianity. The Christians knew that they would have to destroy the influence of these cults if they were to assume uncontested political power. Furthermore, Christian Church fathers felt obliged to denigrate, destroy, and uproot the influence of these cults if they were to maintain any sort of spiritual authority in Rome.

Aphrodite, the mother of the Roman people, was the cosmic manifestation of physical desire. And as a result, the Christians targeted the goddess in order to break her cult's hold over the political imagination of the Greco-Roman world. It was the apostles and the early Church fathers—certainly not the Romans—who taught that the beauty of the female form should be hidden, because it was, in essence, a manifestation of evil.

The Christians taught that women were not creators, but facilitators of the devil and his demons. It was Eve, after all, who had brought sin upon the race of mortals, a concept that was entirely foreign to the goddess-worshipping Greeks.

> The Christian man does not see the female form with his redeemed eyes. His soul is blind to sexual allure.
>
> —Tertullian
> APOLOGY

From the Christian perspective, the power of a woman was her power of attraction. And that power had to be broken. Outlawing the use of drugs by the followers of Dionysus and Aphrodite was just one means of initiating the destruction of classical religion. For centuries, Church fathers taught that sexual attraction was a spiritual crime that could send one to Hell for an eternity. The half-naked dances performed by pagan teenage girls were anathema to the Christians. They engendered desire in the minds of the pagan world and thus inspired the influence of the pagan "demons." As a result, desire became taboo, and the drugs used to promote it became illegal.

The war against western culture started in earnest when the first western women of the Common Era were sent to jail for their use of drugs. The promotion of these anti-drug laws meant that women could be imprisoned for seeking out drugs to induce abortion or to regulate menstruation. Women were cast out of political positions—the oracles who had been giving advice to kings, tyrants and democratic leaders alike—and removed from Christian society. Their temples were destroyed and looted. And even their midwives, who had been such an integral aspect of the ancient world, were persecuted, imprisoned and executed.

The Social Monster

In the midst of this struggle for power, the Christian leadership, under the direction of bishops and prominent priests, created a social monster. They created exorcists, specialist priests trained to perform the delicate task of uprooting paganism by preventing any sort of demonic "possession." The exorcists conducted a ceremony they referred to as the application of "the fires of temptation." It was a secretive mystery, meant to defile young children in such a way as to prevent their possession by pagan gods. And by passing young boys through the fires of sexual temptation, priests reinforced the exclusivity of the Christian mysteries.

In a strange twist of history, the first rape of children by Christian priests was a means of asserting political and social dominance over pagan religions that venerated the beauty of sexual attraction. Christian priests justified this act as the replication of a mystery performed originally by Jesus himself. Ritual child rape was an integral element of early Christian religion.

The leadership of the early Church clearly recognized the value of ritual sodomy as a successful means of rooting out the influence of female allure on pubescent boys. Raping young men was a highly effective means of combating more-popular, sex-centered pagan religions; these mystery rites were meant to prevent young converts from ever following the cults of Aphrodite and Dionysus, but they also established a degree of exclusivity not present in competing mystery cults. When early Christians were born again, they were psychologically unique, as a direct result of the ritual rape they endured.

Chapter 2

The Way

When early Christian priests performed ritual rape, they established a clear means of creating distinct and exclusive groups of followers. It may seem difficult for a modern audience to justify such behavior, but sodomizing boys was a foundational principle of the earliest associations of Christians. In order to understand why such extreme and violent actions could be accepted by a religious organization like that of the followers of Jesus, it is important to understand the earliest Christians as they understood themselves.

The first Christians were not called Christians. They referred to themselves as followers of "The Way." And the non-Christians who populated the Roman Empire in the early years of the Church thought the highly secretive cult was incredibly odd and politically dangerous. When new members joined "The Way," they left their families—with or without children—sold their goods, disavowed any tie to their previous lives, and disappeared from society.

The first Christians were anything but forthcoming. Followers of "The Way" refused to divulge the activities of their most prominent ranks, and believed it was their religious duty to perform their sacraments in isolation from the outside world. Early Christians may have been far from doctrinally united, but they all shared a desire to remain aloof from the Roman authorities who questioned their loyalty to the state.

The first Christians believed that the end of the world was imminent; they prepared for the final apocalypse under the direction of their elders, who taught that the Church was awaiting the slaughter of everyone outside their newfound cult. Descriptions of their doctrines were leaked to the public. As a result, the Romans found Christianity to be culturally and socially disturbing.

The teachings of Christianity sprang from Judaism, an eastern, monotheistic form of worship that was foreign to the Greco-Roman world but nonetheless respected for its age-old traditions. In strict contrast with competing cults, Christianity was openly monotheistic and highly intolerant of competing religions.

Unlike its Jewish predecessor, Christianity became a predominantly anthropocentric form of worship, a peculiarity that prompted the pagan world to consider the Christians to be of the same ilk as "atheists," as Lucian wrote in *Alexander the False Prophet.*

Between Divine and Human

Greeks, Romans and other Mediterranean polytheists believed there was a natural distinction between divinity and humanity and were critical of the fact that the followers of "The Way" venerated an actual man. Whereas Jehovah was never imagined in human form, the Christian god was a perfect man. This worship of humanity drove a deep wedge among Christians, non-Christians and Jews of the early Church era.

Religious strife characterized the rise of Christianity; the Jewish community in Palestine of the first three hundred years of the Common Era viewed the cult as a political threat. On the opposite end of the religious spectrum, the pagan world had nothing but disdain for "The Way" because it considered its followers to be an incredibly impious group that refused to honor the gods. In addition, Christian zealots as early as the first century incited the masses to burn down the city of Rome in order to usher in the end of the world. According to Christian prophecy, the establishment of the kingdom of God required that Rome be burned in a giant conflagration that would herald the return of the founder of "The Way." When Nero blamed the Christians for the large fire of the summer of 64 CE that consumed the majority of the city, he based his conclusions on the well-known anti-Roman political sentiments voiced by the Christians.

The great fire in Rome, followed by war in Judea, created significant dislike among Mediterranean polytheists for the monotheism of Palestine. However, for the Romans the ideology of the Christian community was more difficult to endure than the ancient teachings of Judaism.

Christianity worshipped a masculine divinity, traditionally portrayed as a god who favored a specific ethnic group over all others. Jewish law and the exclusivity of the Jewish religion were actively embraced by the Church and promoted within its own ranks. However, Christianity broke with Judaism over the concept of "eternal reward." Judaism, unlike Christianity, was not a mystery religion in the vein of the cults that populated the Roman world. As a result, it lacked any contentious doctrines that focused on the rewards or punishments of its members in an afterlife; thus Judaism, unlike its Christian cousin, had no interest in proselytizing.

Christianity was born in Palestine, but it propagated itself in pagan environments like Greece and Rome, where it was forced to adapt to and counter the local religions. In an attempt to bolster its membership—something the Jewish nation was not inclined to do—Christianity was forced into a popularity contest with widespread and long-established pagan cults.

As Christianity grew within the agar of classical civilization, it began accumulating wealth from its growing membership. Those entering "The Way" sold their possessions, gave their money to Church leaders, and lived communally with other Christians in relative isolation. The Christian leadership was never held accountable for how they spent their funds.

Church Murders

In order to reinforce the acquisition of the liquidated resources of its followers, the early Church, under the leader-

> Peter is a traitor...In the case of a man named Ananias and his wife, Sapphira, Peter put them to death for failing to surrender the profit from the sale of their land and retaining a little for their own use.
>
> —PORPHYRY ON ST. PETER

ship of St. Peter, murdered members who had been caught withholding funds. In one particularly infamous instance, a married couple, Ananias and Sapphira, were killed by Church leaders, and their deaths were publicized as an example of "the wrath of God" against those who withheld funds from Church elders. The entire incident was written up in the book of The Acts of the Apostles, 5:10, and stood as an example to many generations of Christians.

The harsh way the apostles dealt with Ananias and Sapphira set a precedent; Christians of the second century onward lived in fear of the mortal consequences that might follow any form of disobedience to the men who formed their leadership. The rule of early Christianity was fear; for this reason, non-Christian contemporaries said "The Way" was a cruel and malicious scam perpetrated by its highest ranks with the intent of making them wealthy.

Despite pagan condemnation of the Christian movement as a sham appeal to the ignorant, the growth of Christianity did not diminish. The pagan world claimed Christian popularity was a result of exposing the uneducated masses to a doctrine rooted in fear. Celsus, an ardent critic of the Church, claimed in *On the True Doctrine* that Christian teachers purposely targeted uneducated audiences in order to garner the most followers. The Church burned Celsus' books, because his arguments were perceived to be a threat to Church survival. However, fragments of his books survive as extensive quotations in Christian writings that attempted to refute his dangerous assertions.

In one particularly revealing invective, also in *On the True Doctrine*, Celsus illustrates the dangerously exclusive nature of the early Christian teachers: "A teacher of the Christian faith is a charlatan who promises to restore sick bodies to health, but discourages his patients from seeing a first-class physician with a real remedy for fear superior skill and training will show him up. Thus, the Christian teachers warn, 'Keep away from physicians.' And to the scum that constitutes their assemblies, they say 'Make sure none of you ever obtains knowledge, for too much learning is a dangerous thing: knowledge is a disease for the soul, and the soul that acquires knowledge will perish."

Christianity's abhorrence for pagan education was very much a reaction to its surroundings. As a cult, Christianity was a reverse template of the pagan mystery religions that were so popular in Rome, Greece and Egypt. These mysteries promised, by means of initiation, a knowledge of the afterlife that would enable the novice to experience a fuller existence. Since many pagan cults were centered on the concept of reincarnation, they taught that their knowledge could be used to improve one's lot during the process of being "born again."

ST. PETER, EL GRECO

The Orphics, the Pythagoreans and the Neo-Platonists reinforced the mystery teachings of pagan cults that were popular in the first centuries of the Common Era. In order to combat the wild success of these pagan ideas, the Christians adopted and adapted their core teachings to the novel concept of faith in Jesus.

> And this disease of debauchery [homosexuality] is what men call Eros, making unbridled lust into a god.
>
> —CLEMENT OF ALEXANDRIA
> EXHORTATION TO THE GREEKS

The mysteries of the pagans involved sacraments. The pagans used specific elements and symbols in order to perform their mystery rites; they believed the use of specific drugs under controlled circumstances could facilitate a means of communicating esoteric knowledge to initiates. Christian fathers adopted these sacraments. However, whereas the pagans actively used psychotropic drugs to induce visionary states, the Christians forbade their use and eventually promoted the adoption of a universal sacrament that was drug-free.

Christianity insisted on a drug-free sacrament for one reason. The Christians had created a unique religious concept that had never been advanced by the polytheistic religions of the Mediterranean: they created "doctrine." And doctrine took the place of the wisdom-searching role of the drug-using pagan religious experience. Christian priests didn't need to encourage spiritual discovery, because their doctrines were complete expressions of absolute truth; and what else did a Christian pilgrim need?

Christians bound themselves to a specific ideology. In stark contrast, orthodoxy was never a factor of pagan cult practice. Thanks to the advancement of a universal doctrine, there was no need in Christian circles for an individualized spiritual experience—as would typically be afforded by pagan priests in the administration of psychotropic drugs. In other words, the Christians were not expected to have their own vision of God; they were told exactly what to think.

Insistence on Faith

The concept of "faith" evolved from the Christian drive to universalize doctrine. Faith, or belief in a creed, was never a virtue of the classical world. Greek and Roman pagans never established a single unified faith. Their cults were based heavily on the dynamics of an individual's experience with the divine. For this reason, the pagans never produced orthodox prophets and heretical prophets; they birthed poets.

Faith, homosexuality and virginity were moral creations traceable to the Christian cultural world. Priests and monks derived, propagated and defended these concepts, while common pagans found them to be nothing but troubling; some pagans even considered Christian dogma to be a threat to the survival of civic order.

The Christian creed was very straightforward. Simply stated, the masculine god of the universe became a specific man; this man then established a transcendent standard by which all mortals would be judged as worthy or unworthy of perpetual bliss. There was no place in the Christian creed for the spiritual ecstasy that characterized competing pagan religions. For the Christian, an understanding of the dogma of Christ was the only means of salvation.

Christians were expected to follow a set of Mosaic commands that had been modified by Jesus and his disciples. As Jesus, the apostles and the early Church fathers began elevating specific Mosaic commandments and deemphasizing others, they created guiding principles of the spiritual life that tended to focus on specific cultural values, which sometimes ran contrary to the pagan religions that held sway at the time. For example, the wildly popular cult of Dionysus celebrated an effeminate god who was said to have performed openly homoerotic acts. The Christians emphasized the Jewish prohibition of sodomy, and created the modern concept of "homosexuality" as a form of sexual sin. This disenfranchised a large segment of the pagan world and labeled them as outcasts and moral reprobates.

Furthermore, in response to the popularity of the cult of Aphrodite, which focused upon the beauty of the female form, the Christians outlawed the open celebration of feminine beauty by arguing that sexual appeal was akin to spiritual crime. When Jesus claimed that looking at a woman was a sin, his words were an intentional slap in the face of the Greco-Roman culture that permeated his homeland.

The Christians became increasingly aggressive in the early centuries of the Church and made crimes of the religious acts performed by the pagans. Sexuality became a crime in and of itself. Virginity, as a moral concept, was created by Christian priests in response to pagan celebrations of sexuality. According to the pagans, sex was an act of Nature, and therefore something to be venerated. Their Christian contemporaries argued just the opposite—that sex was a crime.

The Christian drive to control sexual desire was not simply a result of the Mosaic commandments. The Jewish founders of Christianity who modified their Mosaic imperatives did so in order to control the sexuality of women. The Church fathers were interested in controlling female sexuality for one very important reason: the feminine voice expressed by pagan cults prevented the Church from gaining political power in Rome.

Unfortunately, this negative view of women held by Christian authorities helped to establish a need for a doctrinal requirement for sexual "purity." As priests and bishops taught that women and the sexual allure associated with them was a sin worthy of the fires of Hell, they logically developed a means of purging young Christians of these damning desires for sex. The mystery of the catechumen's initiation was a ritualistic form of sodomy, designed by the Church to turn young believers away from the ills of sexual desire.

Chapter 3

Defining Youth

Followers of "The Way" had a very different outlook on life than their pagan neighbors had. Views of women, sex, and puberty were three important examples of the most obvious cultural distinctions that separated Christians from non-Christians. Priests and bishops could sodomize young boys, in part, because of their unique views of youth and sexual maturation.

The Christian world looked upon the pre-pubertal and adolescent years of human life in a very different way from their pagan neighbors. Sexual development, for the Church fathers, was a degrading process, something best covered, hidden and ignored. Because the pagans publicly celebrated and even worshipped the bloom of youth, they found themselves in direct conflict with Church authorities.

The view of adolescence as a period of shame in the life of any individual provided Christian priests with a firmer justification for horrendous sexual acts of "purification" committed against minors. Puberty's physical transformation of young boys into sexually developed young men was interpreted by the Church as an avenue of temptation. Since sexual sin was believed to be spiritually lethal, Christian priests felt justified in using extreme measures to prevent it.

The ritual sodomizing of young boys was undertaken as a response to the pagan veneration of the bloom of youth. However, it wasn't just a movement against youth. It was also an attempt to strike at the very heart of paganism.

Ritual rape committed by the Church was very much an attempt to stifle the veneration of pubertal development, and the potential contribution of young boys and girls to society.

The first time the word "history" was ever uttered, it came from the lips of a teenage girl. The term was not coined by a professor, or a philosopher, or even an adult; "history" is a Greek concept, and it emerged from a culture that worshipped young women, blooming flowers, the cycle of life, and drug-induced ecstasy. Before "history" became "a record of the past" as we know it today, it was a term attached specifically to the inspiration of young women recently initiated into the world of adulthood, drugs and menstruation. The verb "historeo" in Greek simply means to make an inquiry of an oracle, and eventually came to mean any form of investigation.

Two thousand five hundred years ago, "history" initially meant "a question posed to a drug-addled girl-priestess." Not just any question, but the most important question anyone could possibly want to ask. Petitioners traveled great distances to ancient temples where they could submit questions on any topic to an oracular priestess; they asked about government, health, law and even the meaning of life. And so "History" referred to one of these official inquiries posed to any oracle.

Answers given by these priestesses were considered manifestations of cosmic truth. It may be difficult for the modern world to comprehend, but the concept of "history" first denoted a question that only a newly reproductively-capable girl could answer, and only when she was under the influence of a good quantity of drugs.

YOUTHFUL HERMES

The Greeks worshiped music and inspiration, along with desire. As a very influential culture in antiquity, the Greeks believed that music and inspiration would forever outlast the physical existence of any single being; ancient polytheists believed the gods were immortal because they were a part of nature. In other words, the same culture that invented atomic theory, free speech and science believed that poetry and song were expressions of the eternal aspects of the cosmos; music was an immortal presence that could be rationally comprehended by humans, without the necessity of miraculous revelation like that in the New Testament.

Greek religious beliefs centered on the veneration of a group of dancing, poetry-reciting teenage girls. The Muses were the daughters of Memory, and the cult of the Muses was the foundation for all Greek religion. All Greek gods, of both the Olympian and Chthonian types, were portrayed as having some specific relation to the Muses, as either defenders or directors. Their prominence and ritual role as the purifiers of oracular cult participants would indicate a central role of the Muses in the formation of Greek religion. Myth itself, the vehicle of ancient cult, is considered to spring from them.

Educated Young Women

In the pre-Christian West, all religious celebrations centered on a chorus of dancers, young women called Kourai, whose education in astronomy, poetry, music, geometry, biology and medicine provided them with the inspiration needed to guide their society. Ancient altars, burning with the fumes of psychotropic plants, filled these adolescent performers with a sacred "flame" of enlightenment. Greeks from all over the pan-Hellenic world came to observe their dance and breathe in their inspiration.

One of the earliest portrayals of a chorus of oracular Kourai can be found in the Homeric *Hymn to Delian Apollo*. Hymns were sacred songs, composed for different Greek divinities, and were a common form of sacred performance. These religious songs are replete with examples of the power of the ancient chorus. This Homeric hymn contains a beautiful description of the theatrical power of the archaic Greek chorus.

As servants of Apollo, the priestesses of Delos were trained in a peculiar form of divination. Apollo's seers were known for riddling symbolic responses to questions of petitioners, who came to the god to ask for wisdom in specific matters, sometimes personal, sometimes political.

> The Lord [Apollo] whose is the oracle in Delphi neither declares nor hides, but sets forth by signs
> —HERACLITUS
> ON THE UNIVERSE

Apollo was often given the cult title "Loxias," a Greek word that is actually a geometric term and literally means "oblique." That is, the god's responses were nether parallel nor perpendicular to the questions petitioners posed—his priestesses answered questions in an oblique fashion; their answers were askew. According to Heraclitus, a Greek philosopher known for his terse and cryptic statements, the divination of Apollo was a matter for the discerning mind alone, as stated in *On the Universe.*

Apollo's teenage servants, in granting answers to inquiries, never gave direct answers to petitioners. The maidens of Delos may have been frequently misunderstood on this basis, but their philosophy pointed to a profound comprehension of the complex workings of Nature. This makes perfect sense when we consider that these priestesses were schooled in subjects like astronomy, geometry, poetry, music and dance. Their singing was filled with references to natural science.

Regardless of the varying degrees of clarity or obscurity found in their pronouncements, the craft of the oracles harkened back to the most important symbols of Apollo himself, his musical instrument and the weapon for which he was so well known. Greek oracular cults always returned to the basic philosophical principles that characterized the pan-Hellenic worship of Apollo.

The bow and the lyre are the central components of the worship of Apollo Loxias, the oracular god of the Olympians. By means of the "tension" produced by the stringing of the bow, or the plucking of the lyre, the ancient world was able to signify that life's meaning, or harmony, was the result of opposing forces of Nature. Tension became a force for "vision," and the temporary mania of the mantic priestess became the product of universal pressures that pull the material world in opposite directions. In the minds of the priestesses of Apollo Loxias, the bow and the lyre were the greatest gifts for mortals because they held the secret to accessing inspiration.

Poets, therefore, were considered the very mouthpiece of the universe, and their music became the medicine of the healing god Apollo. By means of the bow and lyre, the followers of Apollo were deemed to be capable of providing humankind with a relief from sorrow and pain.

The god's songs, expressed in the voice of the chorus of oracular priestesses, were considered to be an avenue of forgetfulness whereby simple "bread-eaters" could put aside their concerns about death and the cruelty of old age. In a sense, Apollo's bow and lyre provided mortals with a soothing drug for the savage pain of mortal reality.

Scholars of Classics have proposed numerous sources for the inspiration of the oracles of Apollo; some say it was gas fumes and others postulate fasting and sleep deprivation. All of these forms of shamanistic ecstasy are possible explanations for the strange and disturbing behavior of oracular priestesses, but the most probable sources of their odd performances are the arrow toxins found in the religious and medical texts connected with the worship of Apollo. Indeed, it appears that the oracles of Apollo, his "drug-savvy servants," were schooled in the use of snake-derived venoms used in archaic Greece as arrow poisons.

APOLLO WITH ARROWS.

Anyone witnessing the use of such drugs would undoubtedly recognize the madness that the Greeks considered a form of communication with the gods. In fact, the behavior of the person suffering an arrow-poison overdose is similar to the strange public performances of the oracular priestesses of the goddess Rhea, one of the oldest divinatory deities.

The Greeks associated the inspirational "shout" of the intoxicated oracular priestess with the manifestation of divine "vision." The priestesses of Rhea, with their intermittent street performances, in which they terrified onlookers with maniacal yelling, were an important religious element of the ancient world. Such crazy public behavior would not be tolerated today, but two thousand years ago it was considered a necessary and valuable aspect of religious worship; as priestesses ranted at passersby, the public considered their drug-influenced screams and confused utterances to be declarations of the gods.

What Oracles Said

Theatrical performances given by intoxicated priestesses were not just a flight of fancy. In antiquity, the pronouncements of oracles were a constant guard against the excesses of tyrants and aristocrats who labored endlessly to deprive the citizenry of personal liberties. Mantic priestesses were a constant check on the ruling elite, and their oracular utterances protected the citizenry from political abuse; when an oracle of Apollo decreed that a tyrant should be exiled or worse, he was.

The oracle at Delphi commanded the people of Acragas, a Greek colony in southern Italy, to stand together as a unified political group against their abusive tyrant, according to Iamblichus in *Life of Pythagoras*. The very same oracles encouraged the democratic reformer Solon to work with the common Athenians as his political base, rather than just wealthy aristocrats, as Plutarch wrote in *Lives: Solon*. And according to Herodotus in *The Histories*, the Delphic oracle also famously encouraged the Spartans to liberate Athens from the terrible tyrant Hippias.

Priestesses of Apollo, particularly those at Delphi, had the power to sanction the foundation of colonies, prevent or endorse declarations of war, and intervene in legal matters anywhere in the Greek speaking world. Rulers and subjects, rich and poor, flocked to the oracles of Apollo in order to learn the god's will. In this way, ancient priestesses were able to exert tremendous influence on the flow of Greek history. The oracles—these teenage, drug-addled girls—were considered the guardians of western culture; they were the voice of the gods, whose pronouncements consistently favored the development of democracy over aristocratic power.

Even in Sparta, the oracles labored to preserve the rights of the citizens over tyrants. For example, the priestesses of Delphi endorsed reforms under Lycurgus that gave Spartan women considerable freedoms, as Plutarch wrote in *Lives: Lycurgus*.

Before, during, and following the development of the "rule of the people" in Athens of the 5th century B.C.E., oracular priestesses were the first pioneers of free speech. During this archaic period the Greek speaking world came to the conclusion that the voice of a pubescent girl on drugs was the most potent tool for the preservation of personal freedom—they believed these teenage girls were above cor-

TEMPLE OF APOLLO, DELPHI.

These wild images are not the work of wise men or even of the sibyls [oracles].
—PORPHYRY
ON JESUS' PARABLES

ruption, they believed they were amenable to inspiration, and they believed their songs captured the enduring beauty of the creative cosmos.

Christian priests railed against the influence of oracular cults, as the Church competed with Roman, Greek and Egyptian mysteries for members. Ceremonies involving exorcist priests who molested and sodomized young boys were meant to undercut the authority of oracular priesthoods. In fact, the very act of raping a child meant that the same adolescent could never participate in a pagan oracular ritual.

In the minds of the priests who initiated these boys, the act of sodomy drove away the demons, which could no longer tempt their young initiates. Why? Because the pagans taught that participants in oracular ceremonies had to remain unviolated. In this way, the process of raping children became a means of protecting them from the "demons" of other religions, and thereby a necessary evil.

Chapter 4

Feminine Foundations of Civilization

Catholic priests justified the abuse of young children as an attempt to prevent sexually inexperienced youths from ever being possessed by pagan demons. However, ritual rape had another ominous purpose; priests raped young boys in order to prevent them from cultivating any future sexual desire for women. In doing so, they purposely attacked the very foundation of western culture.

Ritual sodomy was not a random act perpetrated as an opportunistic impulse for immediate gratification; it was very much a calculated and doctrinally justified attempt to reshape pagan culture. Ritual rape by Christian priests was designed to undercut the core of pagan philosophy—the very same philosophy that was sponsored by pagan temples, shrines and treasuries.

The Christian hierarchy was well aware of the scaffolding upon which pagan religion was built. By altering views on sexual drive, the Christians attacked the ancient religious paradigm of the natural cosmos as the highest source of good as it was used by the Greeks, Romans and Egyptians.

> Why should you find pleasure in a young girl, pretty and voluptuous?... You fancy that you can sleep safely beside a death-dealing serpent.
>
> —JEROME
> LETTER 128

Every western religion is derived from this single model. There is nothing unique about any of our western forms of worship. The earliest western religions of recorded history can be characterized by their universal use of oracular priests, their veneration of holy sites, their inclusion of a ritual of divine communication, their promotion of special guardians of the divinity, and their use of drugs by priests and prophets.

The unity and universal nature of pagan religion was valuable, because the Greeks and the Romans were able to expand their simple model of religion to create western society itself. Western government, law and education are based in this religious paradigm.

The Church intentionally undermined pagan polytheism in order to establish its own peculiar customs and to defend its institutional abuse of children.

All elements of the classical world, be they social or political, were influenced by pagan religious worship. The principles of democracy, philosophy, art and the scientific method are inextricably connected with polytheistic paganism.

The oracular priestess held the most ancient sacred career. Before there existed male prophets, there were female sibyls. Before male spiritual leaders handed down law codes, women sat in judgment of tyrants.

The oracular priestess was nothing less than the living representative of the immortals: she spoke the gods' words, she sang the gods' songs, and she performed the gods' dances. She was the means whereby immortal principles of life could communicate with humanity. Oracular priestesses weren't just spiritual advisors; they gave medical

JEROME, EL GRECO.

> The sibyl with raving mouth utters things mirthless, unadorned and unperfumed, but with her voice she extends over a thousand years because of the god.
>
> —HERACLITUS
> ON THE UNIVERSE

advice, sanctioned wars, and handed down judgments in the case of extreme crimes.

The intent of classical priestly colleges was to enable these girls to learn a technique whereby they could best reflect the mind of the immortal principles that govern the cosmos—ancient divinities were more like gravity than God. The Orphic Hymns are a complete set of pagan celebrations that feature the use of epithets that assign traits to gods as if they were principles of physics. The Orphic and Hesiodic theogonies do the very same thing. Oracular priestesses celebrated the gods as logical products of Nature.

Priestesses were chosen on the basis of physical and mental attributes that distinguished them from their peers. As representatives of divine beauty, they had to be perfect. They were the most intellectually advanced of the masses; they were the tallest, the most athletic, the most coordinated, and the most graceful. These priestesses were the best dancers and singers of their generations. Any physical or mental blemish disqualified them from candidacy. They were also the most intellectually apt of their peers. The poetry they produced was as elegant as the science they advanced.

Promoting Nature

Oracular priestesses worked to promote the values of Nature and to incorporate them into their own societies. And as defenders of the natural world, they were avowed enemies of tyranny. Before democracy became a reality in 5th century B.C.E. Athens, oracular priestesses promoted democratic virtues like free speech, the protection of artistic exercise, and the research of science.

Oracular priestesses lived and worked at specific holy sites. The locations of oracular temples were important because the ancient world believed a temple's setting reflected the power of the gods. Specific gods or divine powers spoke to people through the oracle, and the oracle was inspired by the natural beauty of the location where the temple was built. Ancient oracular temples were typically situated in places of extreme beauty, surrounded by impressive landscapes—meant to overwhelm both the oracles and those who brought them questions.

The oldest religious sites that were home to oracular cults were caves. Caves were the natural temples of the gods. Within these caves, with their unique acoustics, oracular priestesses absorbed the language of the gods and transmitted it to their contemporaries. These priestesses didn't create song for the sake of entertainment alone; they ministered to the needs of local communities. They established precedents of justice and organization that became the model for the expansion of Greek and Roman culture.

Oracular priestesses served specific gods. However, these gods were not the anthropomorphic representations that modern Christian culture envisions. They were instead the immortal principles of Nature; the ageless and deathless concepts inherent in the natural world.

Some priestesses served the Muses, the goddesses of inspiration. Some served Apollo, the divine, musical voice that—like an arrow shot from a bow—always hit its mark. Other priestesses served Black Night, the earliest oracular divinity, who was herself represented as the divine nourisher of children, or, in the archaic Greek mind, the first and most profound feminine voice of the universe. Some priestesses served Dionysus, the voice of ecstasy and intoxication, the effeminate youth who represented the power of drugs and inner madness. These were the gods they served, and at each temple they emphasized the natural realm of a specific god with their oracular utterances.

Due to their profound popularity, oracular priestesses required their own bodyguards. These young girls often presided in judicial proceedings that involved powerful political and military figures, and they therefore required constant protection from the megalomaniacal, greedy and perverse rulers of city-states and empires who populated the ancient world. These priestesses were so powerful that they could order the execution of kings and generals. Their pronouncements often affected the outcome of wars and the allocation of huge sums of military and civilian resources. It only makes sense then that the ancient world felt they needed personal protection from the wealthy and powerful men who dominated the politics of antiquity.

Those recruited to protect oracular priestesses were usually women and typically employed the most lethal weapons of their time. They used highly poisonous drug concoctions to bring about the swift death of anyone attempting to abuse the oracle. They were trained in the use of bows, and they poisoned their arrows with paralytics derived from snakes, insects and dangerous plants. The presence of these guards during oracular performances lent a genuine solemnity to the ceremonies. Oracular bodyguards carried such lethal weapons that Greek playwrights claimed the priestesses were safe even in the presence of an unshackled male, on trial for the capital crime of murder.

It's important to recognize the fact that early archaic priestesses wielded such powerful weapons because their use of poisons was an example of their ability to exert political force. Pagan priestesses did not just exercise symbolic authority; they actually used deadly force when necessary to promote their own political agenda. The Christian world recognized this tradition.

Unique associations of bodyguards served different gods and their temples

ERECHTHEUM, ATHENS.

across the Mediterranean. These women were popularized with the creation of names used to describe their own proficiencies and duties. For example, the "Wolves" served Aphrodite and were known for their bestial aggression, solitary independence, and unrelenting devotion to the cause. The "Dragons" served the temples of the Muses, were distinguished by their snakeskin-like tattoos, and were known for their assassin's ability, thanks to their expert use of paralytic venoms. The "Sphinxes" derived the name of their association from the Greek word denoting "strangulation" and earned their name by using toxins that would asphyxiate their victims—and of all the ancient oracular guardians, they were probably the most feared.

Most of these guards used their own drugs on themselves in small quantities in order to experience their various mind-altering effects, but they also took these drugs in order to develop immunity. Using such dangerous drugs gave oracular bodyguards a unique, fearsome mystique.

Oracular body guards were called Medusae, the Greek word for "judge" or "protector." In fact, temple guardians originally acted as the enforcement arm of oracular temples. The infamous oracular guardian known as Medusa came from their ranks. The Greeks claimed she could quickly and efficiently paralyze her victims, and warned that the application of her poison to the eyes was all that was needed to finish off anyone attacking the oracle. As a matter of fact, there was a general rule in the ancient world that it was best not to look at the bodyguards of the oracular priestesses—lest one end up on the floor, unable to move.

The Furies were a specific group of Medusae who guarded the oracles of Black Night. As daughters of Night, and sisters of the Fates, the Furies enforced the decrees of the "divine nourisher of children." As a result, they logically had jurisdiction throughout the ancient Mediterranean in cases of crimes committed against family members. When one family member murdered another, the Furies were the special agents who would be sent to take justice on behalf of the dead.

> That the serpent [Draco] is among the chief symbols of the sun is shown by the way its name is formed from derkein, that is, "to see": for they say that this serpent imitates this star's nature with very sharp and always wakeful glance, and that serpents are made to guard temples, shrines, oracles and treasuries on that account.
>
> —MACROBIUS
> SATURNALIA

They were considered Sphinxes and they make numerous appearances in Greek myth and ancient tragedy. Like many priestesses, they ended up with their own cult following and were worshipped in prominent cities.

The Order of Draco was a prominent college of Medusae who defended the personal safety of specific oracular priestesses, particularly those found at the famously important shrine at Delphi. Like the Furies, the followers of Draco established a widespread following of worshippers. The Order of Draco was known for its ability to perform superhuman feats. Their guards were among the most feared.

There were even wars in antiquity that pitted various orders of Medusae against one another. For example, the holy site of Apollo at Delphi was originally presided over by the order of Draco and its oracular priestess. However, the Order of Draco at Delphi was overthrown in a single historically important contest, and a new college of priests and Medusae under the leadership of Apollo was established in their place. The Homeric *Hymn to Delian Apollo* tells how they were overcome with the poison arrows used by Apollo.

The Uses of Venom

The ancient Greek world was well versed in the use of dozens of venomous snake toxins. The Order of Draco was famous for its manipulation of these venoms, but the priestesses of Apollo apparently utilized a species of venom that was unknown to the order. The Greeks mastered the use of neurotoxins, necrotizing venoms, and hemorrhage-producing venoms in both recreational and militaristic settings. The knowledge of these venoms was considered sacred and the recipes for the poisons they used were closely guarded secrets. Oftentimes, the priests and Medusae used code words to represent the species of animals and plants used to craft their potions—and prevent their competitors from acquiring their pharmaceutical formulae. These code names ended up in classical pharmaceutical texts used by physicians. For example, the milky juice of one particular plant was referred to as the "semen of Helios."

The Medusae demanded a form of justice that set the stage for the evolution of the courts in the ancient world. They were an important element of a universal religious system that employed oracular priestesses, built temples in holy sites, and created drug mixtures that were used as sacraments during the initiation of novices. The oracles protected and preserved a religious scaffolding that ultimately formed the basis for western democracy. These religious organizations promoted the cultural ideals upon which the western world created ideas like free speech, liberty and science. The western jury itself derives from the chorus of priestesses who were presided over by the oracular priestess—herself the template for modern judges.

The pagan world associated women's political rights with the protection or guardianship of the female voice. Feminine political expression was conjoined with the power of a woman to produce and nourish offspring. Furthermore, the trigger of the political gun of female power was feminine sexual allure. Therefore, in the pagan mind and in pagan civilization, female sexual beauty was the source of feminine power.

When the Christian world began employing ritual rape in its initiation ceremonies, it did so against the background of the prominent role of women as defenders of free expression. Christian fathers taught that free expression was the enemy of Christian doctrine—after all, from the earliest days of the Church, heresy was anything spoken that was contrary to the central dogma of the founders.

As a result of the link among women, sexual allure, the nourishment of offspring, and free speech, the Christian world denigrated the religious practices of specific "All-Mother" cults that promoted these pagan values. Ritual rape was one way of breaking the link between masculine adherents of these pagan cults and their priestesses, who possessed concrete political power. The Christians knew they needed the head of Medusa to capture the Empire.

Chapter 5

Paralyzing Child Protection

In order to break the pagan religious hold on the mind of the Roman world, the Christians redefined the role of the child-nourisher. Pagans worshipped female gods; they venerated sex. And most especially, the pagan world viewed women as the creative and nourishing source of the cosmos. Church fathers were born into this society, and as a result they knew that they needed to dissociate sexuality from child-nourishing—because the pagans had made the association for centuries.

Christian sexual abuse gave priests an additional tool against the influence of competing religious cults; it allowed them to create a group of exclusive followers who rejected the breast-feeding mother figure as the highest authority. In other words, creating an image of sexual intercourse as a negative and harmful act in the mind of young rape victims reinforced the notion that women were a source of evil, rather than a source of protection.

By attacking the concept of women as Nature's nurturers, the Church asserted a single-minded vision of masculine authority that cut to the quick of the psyche of its initiates. This war against the image of the mothering goddess was dangerous, because it undercut much of the bedrock of civilization—and also gave priests more authority to abuse young boys.

Greek goddesses were very important to the pre-Christian world; without their protections, priests were free to redefine much of Nature.

> Women big with child are a revolting sight.
>
> —JEROME
> LETTER 107

In the Greek cosmogony, Night was the primordial goddess of western civilization. She preceded the Olympians; she preceded all the gods of Greece and Rome. Her original title was "Black Night," and she was the "Nurturer of Children." She was the divine feminine voice that came before anything masculine and echoed across the cosmos. She was the source of civilization. She was, in fact, the only god to whom the masculine leaders of the classical pantheon deferred; Zeus may have led the Greek and Roman worlds to glory, but even he bent the knee to the goddess Night, as seen in Homer's *Iliad*.

The cult of Night reaches into every ancient religious practice of the western world. Hers was the first oracular office. The roots of western medicine lie in the cult of Black Night. The oldest forms of the western jury were generated from her worship. Even democracy can trace its roots back to her worship.

Preserving the Nurturer

The social focus of the cult of Night was the preservation of the child nurturer. Priestesses who served in colleges dedicated to this goddess ultimately served women—not just any women, but women who through the process of pregnancy and delivery fostered the growth of civilization. Gynecology and obstetrics were the first western forms of medicine, because the medicine of women was the basis of ancient agrarian communities.

ARTEMIS, THE MANY BREASTED GODDESS

It's an odd but discernible fact of history that the foundations of western medicine lie in the administration of drugs meant to manipulate the menstrual cycle. The concept of the "cycle" was central to the worship of Night, and since she was a goddess of nature, her worshippers perfected the ability to manipulate female physiology.

> Nemesis... is worshiped as the antidote of arrogance.
> —MACROBIUS
> SATURNALIA

As a mother goddess, Night gave birth to a myriad of immortals whose worship formed the foundation of western civilization. Among her daughters were the Furies, the defenders of the concept of the sacred bonds between relatives. The Furies are featured in the plays of Aeschylus, where they are portrayed as the avenging spirits of a woman killed by her son. Crimes against parents and children were unforgivable. The daughters of Night were divinities who upheld the most basic standard of justice in archaic Greece.

The Fates were also the daughters of Night, and Night was considered to be the only goddess capable of affecting the outcome of a mortal's life as guided by the Fates. Even Olympian Zeus, the King of agrarian civilization, was considered to be subject to the Fates and thus Night as well. The concept of fate provided a balance for the ancient world. The Greeks and Romans believed that life was not a chance occurrence but a song; they believed an individual's life had both purpose and meaning, and that ultimately an individual's existence revealed a greater lesson—be it good or bad.

One of the more striking daughters of Night was Nemesis. Nemesis meant "retribution," particularly a form of retribution provoked by verbal hubris—words spoken in pride. The concept of hubris is foreign to Christian culture, but in antiquity, where the idea of original sin did not exist, hubris was the greatest of crimes. To perform an act of violence out of pride, or a lack of compassion for the victim, was considered the greatest act of impiety possible. Hubris was ultimately a crime against Nature itself. And any form of spoken hubris, or malicious arrogance, was considered punishable by the great goddess Nemesis.

The enforcement of justice for oral crimes was a unique concept. The fact that a human being could be held responsible for spoken words in a divine cosmos was fundamental to Greek and Roman religion. Just as life had meaning, as woven together by the Fates, so did an individual's words ultimately demand a form of divine justice in order to provide meaning and purpose to existence. In other words, a person was held responsible for every word ever pronounced in life, and punishment for pride was always perfectly fitting.

The Furies, the Fates and Nemesis show us that the cult of Night was focused on the implementation and enforcement of justice. That is, the earliest Mediterranean cults were centered upon the establishment and preservation of a legal standard that facilitated the smooth operation of agrarian society. This form of justice was distinctly feminine in nature, and was directly linked with the creative power of the female voice. Stated simply, feminine justice had a voice in the protection of family members, particularly one's own children.

Over time, the cult of Night was assimilated by the worship of Aphrodite. The goddess of allure absorbed the functions of the great mother goddess and became the child-nourishing immortal of the Greek pantheon. Aphrodite was given numerous epithets that came to reflect her expanded role. For example, in some parts of the Mediterranean she was worshiped as Aphrodite-Ourania, a goddess of early cosmic origin who, like Night, controlled the great vastness of the vault of the heavens and was an oracular divinity.

The enforcement branch of the oracular cult of Aphrodite was the association of priestesses known as the Wolves. These specially trained girls established a reputation for rigorously upholding the demands and prophecies of the oracular priestesses of Aphrodite. The cult, which was spread across the Near East as well as the Greco-Roman world, had tremendous political power, and the Wolves were charged with the task of ensuring that the will of the oracle was carried out. The Wolves managed transitions of political power and ensured that tyrants were replaced by more democratically minded rulers.

> A woman should associate with her own sex; she should not know how to play with boys, no, she should be afraid to do so.
>
> —JEROME
> LETTER 128

The Wolves typically followed the lead of the oracle at Delphi; they promoted the destruction of tyrants and the preservation of rightful monarchs who would presumably rule with more fairness, since they were not usurpers. The stories of Romulus and Remus, and Miletus, are two examples of the attempts by the wolves to protect the innocent and establish political order, given by Livy in *Ab Urbe Condita* and Antonius Liberalis in *Metamorphoses*.

What the Wolves Did

The best example of the intervention of the Wolves in the political affairs of the ancient world can be seen in the early days of the establishment of the dominance of Rome in Italy. Based on the prophecies of their own sibyls, the Wolves supported a political movement that placed the Latin-speaking peoples at the forefront of Italic power. One Wolf in particular was made famous by protecting the offspring of a priestess of Vesta, whose children were fated by oracular prophecy to become the founders of Rome. This particular she-wolf, as an agent of Aphrodite, literally nourished the children when they had been left for dead by their grandfather, the king of Alba Longa.

The Wolves undertook the assignment of protecting Romulus and Remus because the oracular sibyls had prophesied that the boys would eventually found the city of Rome; in addition to this, the children of this priestess of Vesta were considered to be the descendants of Aphrodite herself—in the form of the Roman Venus.

According to the most reputable Roman historians, the she-wolf nurtured the children with her own breast milk. This is interesting because the Wolves were actually unmarried girls, who would not have been able to lactate naturally, due to the fact that they were never pregnant while in the service of the goddess. However, they actively ingested reptilian toxins that we now know bind to prolactin receptors, thus enabling them to develop active mammary tissue and then lactate. As a result of their chemical regimen, many young Medusae were called upon to serve as the wet nurses of royalty and prominent citizens of antiquity.

The Wolves thus indirectly guided political power in the archaic Greek world. Their actions not only pushed Greek civilization toward a more democratic form of governance, but also reinforced an adherence to the principles of justice that came to characterize western jurisprudence; their feminine political voice heralded the earliest jury trials of the western world.

As Christianity came to power, Christian bishops recognized this gender-specific connection of oracular cults—with their female priestesses—and the exercise of a strong judiciary. Church fathers of the 2nd through the 4th centuries understood the dominant role of the feminine voice in the administration of justice in pagan culture. Bishops, priests and monks realized that they needed to change the basis of western justice in order to promote a Christian form of government. In other words, the leaders of the Church recognized that political power in Rome could only be gained if they were able to undercut the feminine voice as the basis of western judgment and morality.

The strong feminine drive to provide justice to one's offspring was a cornerstone of many ancient cults. When the Christian hierarchy overthrew this model of conduct, it facilitated the breakdown of the protec-

SHE WOLF
NURSING FOUNDERS OF ROME.

tion of minors in Rome. Whether it was intentional or not, denigrating the female as the protector of children made it easier for priests to continue abusing children.

The rise of Christianity to a place of political power and prominence was accompanied by the purposeful diminution and ultimate destruction of the idea that the creative, nurturing female was a source of justice. In order to most thoroughly undercut the political authority of the cult of Aphrodite, and others like it, the Christian hierarchy stabbed at its very heart: the worship of the feminine drive to protect their young. This paved the way for the unmitigated abuse of children.

Chapter 6

Creating Homosexuals and Whores

Christianity didn't just undercut the authority of women as the rightful protectors of children; it took the additional step of ensuring against any sort of concerted feminine reaction to child abuse within the Church by entirely vilifying the role of women in society. Priests facilitated the rape of children in the early centuries of the Common Era by declaring women--and even femininity itself--to be criminal.

The modern notions of the "whore" and the "slut," like the concept of the "homosexual" as distinct from the "heterosexual," are Christian inventions. Early Christian Church leaders intentionally stigmatized women, homosexuals and even drug use, in order to advance a political agenda that fostered the protection and preservation of ritual sodomy.

SATYR, PRAXITELES

The Christian hatred for homosexuals was no less vehement than its native misogyny. For example, Christian authorities are the first sources from the ancient world to refer to homosexual men as "diseased," as Clement of Alexandria did in his *Exhortation to the Greeks*.

> Do not indulge in a passion for the theater, where the actors put on indecent spectacles full of every kind of shameless obscenity, and effeminate men perform wild dances.
>
> —CYRIL
> ADDRESSING PAGAN CUSTOM

As Christianity grew, it became more politically unified. Early Church fathers of the second, third and fourth centuries created a distinct political platform. Priests and bishops used this platform to advance the Christian cause along with their own political power. The ultimate goal was to gain religious legitimacy within the Roman state. Ultimately, the Christian political platform led to the destruction of all competing pagan religions.

What was the first Christian political platform? It was very simple. It contained three planks--or three prohibitions: no drugs, no homosexuals and no female political voice.

The three political prohibitions of early Christianity were a peculiarly brilliant combination of traditional legal authority and biblical spiritual morality. Each prohibition targeted a specific group of political rivals. These three groups were active in disseminating and fostering the growth of pagan religion and pagan political power. The prohibitions targeted theatrical forms of entertainment, the use of drugs in religious ritual, and members of the medical community who practiced feminine medicine.

In short, the early Christians took up political causes meant to outlaw drug use, homosexuality, and female political power.

Christians as early as the apostles argued against the use of drugs. The use of drugs by pagans as a form of holy sacrament was considered anathema. In fact, the term "idolatry" was coined as a means of making pagan drug use illicit and illegal. Pagans burned psychotropic plants on incense altars in enclosed religious spaces. These pagan worshippers became intoxicated in the presence of the cult statue and believed this allowed the god represented by the statue to speak to them personally. The process of animating the temple statue was considered "theurgy" and was as ancient as Greco-Roman civilization itself.

The early Christians called theurgy and its practitioners "sorcerers" and "idolaters." The concept of "idolatry," as a native Western concept--not of the Eastern or Jewish traditions--did not exist in antiquity until the rise of Christianity as a political entity. The pagans in Greece, Egypt and Rome never actually worshipped statues; they believed instead that their art was a conduit through which religious observers could become closer to the natural powers of the universe. Drugs derived from plants and animal toxins were considered Nature's vehicle for enhancing this cosmic communion.

The pagan practice of theurgy produced inspired oracular priestesses. These oracles had political power, whereby they were able to influence the declaration of wars, the foundation of colonies, and the creation of legal pronouncements. Oracles maintained a close check on tyrants and tyrannical states, and occasionally ordered the death of kings who overstepped their natural bounds. The oracle also supported the reforms of Lycurgus, which gave Spartan women more freedom than that possessed by the women of Athens; Thucydides wrote of this in *History of the Peloponnesian War*. Oracles also defended free speech, particularly in the case of artists and performers.

These oracles had tremendous political power, and the early Christians considered them a direct obstacle. The Christian effort to end pagan drug use was the first plank in their political platform. The first drug war was an idea that originated in the minds of bishops and priests who desired power.

> Bring forward some one or other of those persons who are supposed to be god-possessed, who by sniffing at altars inhale a divine power in the smell.
>
> —TERTULLIAN
> APOLOGY
> ABOUT FUMIGATIONS

> We [Christians] have nothing to do, in speech, sight or hearing, with...the shamelessness of the theater...
>
> —TERTULLIAN
> APOLOGY

Controlling the Theater

The second plank within the Christian political platform was the assertion of control over pagan theatrical entertainment. Public spectacles, theater, drama, performances and parades were all integral parts of pagan society. These performances were rooted in pagan religion. The ideals of democracy, western education and even the scientific method were all ultimately derived from these public performances. The Greeks and Romans celebrated their artists, but the Christian fathers understood that public performance solidified and reinforced pagan political values. If the Christians were ever going to establish a foothold in ancient government, they would need to uproot these forms of entertainment. As a result, early Christians targeted the celebrations of Dionysus, or Bacchus, the god of the theater.

Dionysus was a notoriously effeminate god. He was given the Greek name "gynomorph," which meant something like "male with female attributes." As the originator of the theater, Dionysus was the patron of public criticism. The modern concept of free speech finds its origins in the performance of ancient tragedies, where playwrights were free--under the protection of religion--to criticize the government. This freedom was a threat to the establishment of Christian rulers, who refused to brook such openly public criticism.

Dionysus was a homoerotic entity. He performed openly homosexual acts. So when the Christians targeted theatrical entertainment, they logically targeted gay men and women as well. The very term "homosexuality" is a Christian invention of the Common Era. The term does not exist in either the Greek or the Latin language. The Greeks and Romans did not believe in the existence of "homosexuals." They thought instead that any person could reasonably choose to have sexual intercourse with either gender. In the pagan mind, there were no "homosexuals" but just people who had sex. Sexual unions between the same sex were not distinguished from those between the opposite sexes. Sex was sex, and it had nothing to do with the "orientation" of an individual.

The Greeks and Romans were not concerned that their greatest heroes were "homosexuals." They knew that Achilles and Hercules enjoyed sex with both genders, and never distinguished them on the basis of these practices.

For Christianity to be able to uproot the foundations of theatrical entertainment, they were forced to attack the cult of Dionysus. Since Dionysus promoted same-gender intercourse, this became a target for zealous priests. Early Christianity created the western concept of "homosexuality" and promoted its war on gay people in order to curtail the influence of public entertainment. In doing so, it used the Jewish holy books as justification. Homosexuals were deemed "godless" and were actively imprisoned and killed.

The third plank in the early Christian political platform was an attack on female health care. For centuries before Christianity, colleges of oracular priestesses supported the training of women physicians who practiced obstetrics and gynecology. Roughly one-third of women died in childbirth, so midwives and female doctors were a valued part of society.

Midwives were directly connected with female religious offices that held political power in the ancient world. Therefore, Christian bishops and priests targeted their drug use as a means of curtailing the female political voice. As a result, Christianity prohibited the use of drugs by female doctors and asserted control over reproductive medicine.

> There are [pagan] women who, by medicinal draughts, extinguish in the womb and commit infanticide upon the offspring yet unborn.
>
> —FIRMICUS MATERNUS CONDEMNING WOMEN FOR PERFORMING ABORTIONS

One of the ways the Christian Church outlawed the long-established practices of midwives was by declaring them "prostitutes," or supporters of sexual promiscuity. The English word "pornography" comes from the early Christian drive to outlaw the artistic depiction of nudity or sexual acts. Christian priests considered nudity and sexual freedom to be the result of the pagan failure to control the dress and public appearance of women. As Christians rose to power, the artistic representation of the human form became a spiritual crime and "pornography" was born. Obscenity became a factor in the creation of art, and for the first time in Greco-Roman history, artists lost their protection as sacrosanct individuals--something given to them by the oracles.

Pagan drug users were arrested, incarcerated, and had their possessions confiscated. The money from the sale of their property was absorbed by the Church. Homosexual men and women were deprived of any civic rights and were even imprisoned, tortured and killed. Women who used drugs to induce abortions were declared servants of the devil, and were zealously persecuted.

As Christianity gained a foothold in the ancient state, it drove drug users, homosexuals and women with political influence to the periphery of society. This made room for bishops and priests to assert their own spiritual, social and political authority, the motive for which was likely the desire for power. But most importantly, it allowed them to continue proselytizing with the goal of creating a highly exclusive group of followers whose understanding of things like sex, drugs and music would foster the promotion of Christianity.

Chapter 7

Political Power and Pornography

Changing the way the world looked at sex facilitated the activities of sodomizing priests while undercutting the political role of women in society. But when priests denigrated women, they also brilliantly paved the way for asserting control over artistic expression—and thus the flow of information in society.

The naked teenage girls known as the Graces may have been a favorite topic of the Greeks and Romans, and the same image would someday become a favorite topic of Renaissance artists, but depictions of these three girls disappeared after the rise of Christianity to a place of political power. For Christian priests trying to sodomize the desire for sex out of young boys, depictions of nude, blossoming teenage girls were nothing less than a form of self-indictment.

A naked teenage girl was early Christianity's worst devil. In the first four hundred years of the Common Era, Christianity created the concept of "pornography," and boldly condemned any sort of naked rendering of the human form. Until the time that Christianity gained true political power, the classical world worshiped young female divinities. Most of the pagan goddesses assumed a single form: the "kore," a teenage

THREE GRACES, POMPEII

> Look, too, at other of your images – little figures of Pan, naked girls [korai], drunken satyrs; and obscene emblems, plainly exhibited in pictures, and self-condemned by their indecency...We declare that not only the use, but also the sight and the very hearing of these things should be forgotten.
>
> —CLEMENT OF ALEXANDRIA
> EXHORTATION TO THE GREEKS

girl at the peak of her physical and intellectual bloom. And when the Greeks and Romans depicted this kore, they depicted her naked.

Christianity, as a religious cult, developed as a reaction to its cultural environs; the faith of the followers of The Way was a visceral response to the pagan world in which the cult initially flourished. Although Christianity was a perfect reflection of the mystery cults that influenced its development, it strove to appear to be everything that paganism was not; Christians tried desperately to distinguish their mystery cult from the mystery cults that had already been long established in the ancient world. The invention of "pornography" enabled them to make a clean break with the pagan world and its ancient traditions.

The concept of "pornography" was created by the Christian world in order to best deal with the problem of the widespread veneration of young teenage goddesses, or korai. The Greeks and the Romans used the term "porneia" to refer to the exchange of money for sexual favors; the term simply meant prostitution, without a harsh moral overtone. However, the Christians adopted the term and applied it to pagan religious rituals that involved naked statues—specifically the representations of young, teenage girls. As a result, "porneia" took on a distinctly moral connotation, and the concept of "pornography," the visual representation of the naked human form, evolved from it.

When the Christians advanced the idea of "pornography," they labeled Greco-Roman art as the source of all idolatry. Nude representations of gods and mythological figures were ubiquitous in the classical world. For centuries, travelers to Greece and Rome from Asia and Africa made note of the many works of art that decorated public and private spaces, but the Christians were the first social group to be uniformly outraged by such depictions of the human form. Before Christianity was the state religion, universal censorship was unimaginable. After the rise of bishops to places of political authority, widespread censorship became a reality. Christian priests targeted the worship of the kore, and in order to blot it off the pages of history they focused on making the artistic depiction of the teenage goddesses illicit and illegal.

Semele was the model kore; as a divine kore, she is perhaps the most illustrative example of the immortal power of youth. Semele was the human mother of Dionysus, the god of wine, vision and ecstasy, and she was ultimately deified. Greek poets tell us she was the daughter of Cadmus, the king of Thebes, and his wife Harmonia, the daughter of Aphrodite herself.

Greek myth presents Semele as a nubile post-pubertal girl, whose beauty and personal grace overwhelmed the inhabitants of her father's native Thebes. As her young body began developing the attributes of a woman, Semele garnered the attention of the chief of the gods himself. Unable to restrain himself, Zeus impregnated the young girl with divine offspring, Dionysus—the son of a god. And Semele, with the growing fetus inside her, danced in an other-worldly manner on the forested mountains and grassy hilltops of northern Greece. Her grace was even augmented by her pregnancy, and the dancing, celebratory teenage mother-to-be became a powerfully iconic image for the Greeks and Romans.

APHRODITE

Ecstatic Semele

In her fits of ecstasy, Semele led the Greek choruses that sang hymns

> Such strength had art to beguile that it became for amorous men a guide to the pit of destruction.
>
> —CLEMENT OF ALEXANDRIA DISCUSSING THE FOLLOWERS OF APHRODITE

to the pagan gods. She celebrated the korai, like Athena, Aphrodite and the Muses, and sang of their immortal beauty. Legend has it that Semele never experienced the birth of her own child, because of her desire to experience Zeus in all his unfiltered glory. She asked the god to come to her bed in his divine form—rather than cloaked as a mortal—and as a result of his willingness to give her what she wanted, she was consumed by the fire of his immortal lightning.

Zeus removed Dionysus from the burning body of his young mother before he could be destroyed. Although Semele was killed, her devotees and the poets who embellished her myths claimed that she, as a mere mortal, celebrated a great triumph over all other mortals as well as the gods. How so? As a simple girl, she drew down from heaven the greatest power of the cosmos, and for a brief moment in time was able to experience pure, unadulterated divinity. Such an honor placed her, as a mortal, in the foremost ranks of humanity. After her death, Semele was celebrated as a burnt offering to the gods and was given the name Thyone, which means something like "sweet smelling offering to the gods."

By the second and third centuries of the common era, Semele's cult following attracted the particular ire of the Christian Church fathers, and her image was therefore actively desecrated by the Christian monks, priests and bishops, who declared the representation of youthful girls to be immoral. The priests of The Way hated the stories of Semele's youthful beauty, and they loathed her offspring Bacchus, but they especially disliked her power of attraction.

As someone who was able to draw down, or attract, the highest form of god from the heights of heaven, Semele demonstrated a power that was clearly unsettling to the Christians. Her voice was the voice of generations of young women, and the Christian priesthood clearly felt threatened by its potential political influence. After all, the celebrants of Semele and Dionysus became the very same oracles who claimed the Christians were not interested in spirituality but instead craved political domination—an earthly kingdom. Even as Christianity struggled to assert itself in the 4th century, the oracles warned of their own imminent demise at the hands of its male-only priesthood. And as it turns out, they accurately predicted their own violent persecution at the hands of the Church.

The invention of pornography, like the creation of anti-drug legislation in the third and fourth centuries, was a brilliant means of undermining the pagan religions that competed with the cult first known as The Way. Up until the time of the rise of the Christian Church as a western political force, there were no limits on the portrayal of the human form. After the bishops secured their own legitimacy and promoted the rise of Christian Roman emperors, nudity became a moral and spiritual crime—much like using drugs—and artists ceased rendering the potent image of the young girl goddesses that were so prevalent in the ancient world.

By stifling the creation of artistic depictions of post-pubertal teenage girls, the Christian hierarchy effectively quashed public discourse relating to the authority of the divinely feminine voice. The figure of the female as creator dropped out of western society, and as people stopped seeing representations of the power of the divine feminine, they were more easily funneled into the only alternative—namely the masculine, Christian god.

For the Greeks and Romans, the portrayal of the natural power belonging to a blossoming youthful girl, like Semele, was a reminder of the relevance of femininity for the makeup of the cosmos, and hence human governance. For the Christians, the destruction of this form, by means of the invention of the concept of "pornography," was an incredibly effective way of stifling the role of women in society and reinforcing the denigration of women in the minds of their initiates.

Chapter 8

Religious Hot-Boxing

Outlawing depictions of nude goddesses assisted in the devaluation of pagan religious ideals, but the socially transformative capacity of women did not reside in ancient art alone. Many of the cults with which Christianity competed employed the use of botanicals and animal-derived toxins as sacramental drugs that were meant to effect a mental change within the ranks of their initiates. These drugs promoted the very ideals that the Christian priests were attempting to curtail.

Clement of Alexandria, an early Church authority, joined the idea of drug use with spiritual ignorance in his *Exhortation to the Greeks*. Clement also vehemently targeted the worship of Aphrodite and Bacchus as two of the sources of mystery initiations concerned with the celebration of sexuality by means of drug use. In one passage Clement even claims that intoxication with drugs predisposes people to perform homosexual acts.

Tertullian, in *De Spectaculis*, was even more aggressive than Clement in his condemnation of the cults of Aphrodite and Bacchus. In one short passage, he attempted to draw a connection among demon possession, drug use, theater and homosexuality—while demanding hate from his fellow Christians: "But Venus and Bacchus do very well together, demons in drunkenness and lust, two yoke-devils sworn to either's purpose. So the theatre of Venus is also the house of Liber...Those features of the stage peculiarly and especially its own, that effeminacy of gesture and posture, they dedicate to Venus and Liber, wanton gods, the one in her sex, the other in his dress...You, O Christian, will hate the things, when you cannot but hate the authors of them."

If Christian authorities peached so vehemently against drug use in Rome, how did the pagans use drugs in their ceremonies? The majority of the time, they employed the act of fumigation. That is, cult officials burned botanicals on public altars where members participated in ancient theurgical rituals. People would inhale the smoke of incense altars and thus interact with the cult statue. Those who performed these rituals reportedly listened to the gods as they spoke through their cult statues.

Fumigation is the oldest form of western religion. Fumigation was the reason the ancient world built temples; it was the motivation behind the design of the altar. Fumigation drove ancient religion from the cave to the sanctuary. It is the reason we have places of worship.

What is at the heart of fumigation? It's all about plants, animals and Nature. Fumigation is the simple process of burning botanicals in order to facilitate their inhalation. It is the precursor of pipe smoking.

The first fumigation was performed in caves, where priests and priestesses burned psychotropic plants, inhaled the fumes created by this combustion, and envisioned the gods. In these caves, religious worshipers sang songs, danced and experienced religious awe—all under the influence of potent drugs. Western religion, drama, history and philosophy were all born from this experience.

Fumigation is not much different from the modern phenomenon known as hot-boxing, in which people sit in an enclosed space, like an automobile, and get high off of primary and secondary smoke. Fumigation, like hot-boxing, is the continuous inhalation of psychotropic

> These unclean spirits, or demons, as revealed to Magi and philosophers, find a lurking place under statues and consecrated images, and by their breath exercise influence as of a present God: at one while they inspire prophets, at another haunt temples...
>
> —FIRMICUS MATERNUS ON FUMIGATIONS

fumes. It is far more intense than simple smoking, and can even be deadly due to the heightened potential of overdose. The benefit of fumigation over simple smoking is the ability to set context. Temple structures were designed with this fact in mind. Creating a space in which a worshipper could experience the gods while breathing in psychoactive substances is an important part of temple architecture.

As western religious rites moved out of caves, they found a home in temples built to facilitate the botanically influenced religious experience. In ancient temples, artists designed specific representations of the gods—the natural forces of the universe—in order to enhance and focus the religious experience.

The Egyptians, like the Greeks and Romans, possessed a long tradition of inhaling drugs in order to perceive the divine world through the artistic representations of sculptors and painters. And like the Greeks and Romans, Egyptian priests and priestesses functioned as oracles.

Statues and Altars

Inside ancient temples, artists typically erected cult statues in the vicinity of incense altars. Incense altars were essentially large barbecues, upon which a large quantity of plant and animal matter could be burnt. The most common example of the enclosed religious structure with its accompanying incense altar is found in the Jewish tradition. The first tabernacle, found in the writings of Moses, was a structure built to facilitate the process of fumigation, or religious hot-boxing.

Jewish priests burned a compound mixture of botanicals within the tabernacle, but prohibited the compounding or burning of the same incense mixture outside of their religious tent. Commoners were forbidden from replicating the mixture, but priests were free to burn it on a daily basis, much like their Greek, Egyptian and Roman counterparts. Jewish priests burned this incense in the area of the tabernacle where they taught that the presence of their god could be experienced. The process of experiencing the Hebrew god, like that of other Mediterranean cultures, was potentially deadly. According to legend, Jewish priests tied a rope around one of their feet—in case they were "overwhelmed" by the god-experience and needed to be dragged from the tabernacle into the open air.

The Greeks and Romans, the founders of western civilization, the inventors of medicine, democracy and the scientific method, perfected the art of fumigation. They performed their rites in small enclosed spaces within the innermost sections of their temples. They performed these rites on initiates who were prepared, by means of fasting and bathing, to receive a vision of the gods.

Some psychotropics used in religious services were so common that they acquired nicknames akin to our modern street names for drugs. For example, marijuana was called "Star," "Spider," and "The Stammerer," as reported by Dioscorides in *De Materia Medica.* The imagery surrounding the drug incorporated itself into the religious myths surrounding the worship of specific gods. The worshippers of Aphrodite and the prophets of Osiris and Bacchus typically used cannabis. The temples of Aphrodite in Cyprus burned their holy incense day and night, all year round. Aphrodite's religious botanicals apparently put her worshippers in the spirit to worship the goddess of desire, and comprehend the significance of the stars.

When mixed with other botanical products, psychotropic plants formed the active ingredients of the compound mixtures of "holy incense" that were used to facilitate the ancient religious experience. The bases for these special drugs were compounded by specific cult adherents. For example, the priestesses of Vesta in Rome were known for the pharmacological substance they made that was used as a drug base throughout the Mediterranean. Only the vestals could reproduce the recipe. The cooperative use of pharmaceu-

PRIESTESS

ticals in the ancient world unified disparate Mediterranean cults, whose practices were dependent upon their ability to maintain the proper drug mixtures, custom designed for their specific practices.

Divine Possession

The pagans considered the drug-induced experience brought about by fumigation to be a form of divine possession. Greeks, Romans and Egyptians believed drugs facilitated a means of communication with the gods. When consuming, or breathing in their drugs, ancient cult practitioners believed they were consuming a natural element of the gods themselves. Once the basic essence of a god was consumed—in the form of a plant- or animal-derived toxin—the religious observer was then able to visualize the actual presence of the god or goddess in the cult statue. They called this practice "theurgy" and they considered it a natural form of possession. The Greek word for "divinity" is "daimon," and thus the practice—through the influence of the Christian cultural lens—became known as demon possession.

When the Christians began a politically motivated campaign against pagan cults like those of Aphrodite and Dionysus, they undertook a propaganda war against the pagans by specifically targeting the terms used by pagan priests. The Christians claimed the pagans were openly promoting "demon possession," which they condemned as an act sanctioned and promoted by the devil himself.

In his *Apologeticus*, Tertullian was quick to point out that Socrates' demon first attacked him as a child. In this famous "Apology" the early Church father claimed that pagan fumigations facilitated a form of demon possession that made them sexually aroused. This is probably not that far-fetched, considering that the pagans frequently used botanicals with aphrodisiac qualities. In the same section of this work, Tertullian unwittingly reveals to his audience that the mysterious name "Dionysus" is actually derived from the Greek words for Zeus (god) and Knissos (the smell of burning botanicals that comes from pagan altars). In other words, Dionysus is the god that makes one horny by means of mania-inducing fumigations—and he had actual horns as well. This meshes well with the ancient concept that Bacchus always leads his followers to Aphrodite, the goddess of sexual desire.

As negative propaganda against pagans began taking hold, priests and bishops created a distinct environment of fear; they labeled pagans as drug-using children of Lucifer, and successfully branded them as moral reprobates. As their own ranks became frightened by pagan practices, and figures like the western witch were born, Christians reacted by creating a spiritual antidote to the pagan practice of demon possession.

In response to the fear generated within the ranks of Christianity—created by the Christian hierarchy itself—bishops and priests invented a ceremony, the performance of which was said to prevent the pagans from inducing demon possession. In what appears to be a twisted bit of history, the Christian priesthood used pagan theology in a horrifically opportunistic way.

The pagans taught that sexual purity of their oracles was a prerequisite for theurgical performances. That is, young pagan priests and priestesses needed to be sexually "pure" or "innocent" if they were to be used as oracles—or possessed by the gods. They could not be approached in a sexual manner during their moments of drug induced inspiration; for the pagans believed that the gods would not be willing to possess a person who was sexually violated—in any manner. As a result, Christian exorcists derived a ritual in which they molested and sodomized young children, in order to guarantee that these same youths could never participate in pagan rituals.

> The breath of demons and angels achieves the corruption of the mind in foul bursts of fury and insanity, or in savage lusts, along with every kind of delusion.
>
> —TERTULLIAN ON THE RESULTS OF FUMIGATION

The Christian priests who performed this ritual abuse became known as "exorcists," and the "temptation of fire" they administered to young boys became a foundational means of entry into the early Christian Church. Christian priests first ritually abused young boys in order to drive them away from pagan social and religious circles. The rite became popular, widespread, and earned the ire of pagans throughout the Mediterranean.

TEMPLE OF SIBYL

Chapter 9

Reinforcing Rape with Sobriety

Catholic priests sodomized young boys in order to drive them away from the pagan mysteries that competed for their attention. However, the Church was well aware that the rigid indoctrination and rape of new members would exert control within its own ranks but could never prevent people outside the Church from condemning such actions.

Pagan temples were the source of pagan education, and educated pagans roundly condemned the Christians for a host of perceived sexual crimes. In order to stop the pagans who belonged to these temples—and those who were educated in the classical tradition—from accusing their priestly ranks of abuse, Church fathers waged a concerted effort to shut down pagan religious practices. The pagan use of drugs was widespread and universal, and therefore a convenient commonality that could be turned as a weapon against the most popular temples of the day.

In what appears to be an unexpected twist of history, the first effort to prevent drug use in the ancient world was directed by Church officials whose focus on prohibition directly facilitated their ability to sodomize children without fear of prosecution.

The first drug war had its inception in the third and fourth centuries of the Christian era. Drugs were never illegal in the pre-Christian world. The Greeks and Romans used them frequently; they used drugs for religious, medical and recreational purposes, and they never outlawed them.

PARTHENON

The only time the classical world ever legislated against the use of drugs was in the case of murder; drugs, like daggers or swords, could be illegally used to kill. But the use of drugs in all other ways was fully supported by the law.

Prohibition did not exist in the ancient world. Before the rise of Christianity to political power, nobody was ever incarcerated for using drugs. Ancient city-states never jailed drug users or imposed any sort of fine for drug use. There were no drug enforcement squads, and nobody ever had property confiscated on the basis of drug use.

The first drug war was directly linked to the rise of Christianity to a place of political prominence. The initial western attempt to make drugs illegal, and illicit, was taken up by priests and bishops, who wanted to use new anti-drug laws to disenfranchise pagans with government positions.

The first drug war was no slight matter. The Christians incarcerated so many people for drug offenses that Roman prisons quickly became overcrowded. Family members of the jailed had to provide food for their own relatives; there was no money to feed the huge influx of newly made drug offenders. Prison conditions were horrendous, and the pagan world complained that the method of housing prisoners was unjust.

Ancient drug users of the Christian era were also executed. They were roughed up by roving gangs of Christian monks, who by imperial decree exercised unlimited authority and jurisdiction over local law enforcement officials. Christian pseudo-law enforcement agents forced their way onto large estates owned by pagans, and assaulted them on the basis that they had been making incense offerings to their gods—incense that the bishops had expressly outlawed; these pagans were jailed and their land and property were confiscated and turned over to the Church. In this way, the bishops multiplied their funds exponentially, and the drug war provided a constant source of funds for the expansion of the priesthood.

Pagans caught using drugs in their homes were subject to swift prosecution; many of them made formal requests to local law enforcement authorities, but their pleas were not of any effect. For, as local magistrates explained, drug enforcement squads held overwhelming moral authority due to their endorsement by the bishops—who themselves were very much in control of the policies made by Christian emperors. This moral authority, and its staunch support by the Christian population, guaranteed that strict drug enforcement was an unquestioned policy.

The first drug war was carried out with extreme zeal. Christian monks and priests painted pagan drug users as the children of the devil and moral reprobates. Pagans who burned incense in celebration of the ancient gods were stigmatized. Christian teachers spread the idea that pagans who used drugs were irredeemably evil, and were suspected of committing terrible sexual crimes and murders. Drug users were blamed for many of the social problems of antiquity, and their stigmatization by the Christians served to facilitate violent policing of drug offenses.

Ancient drug enforcement authorities relied upon the testimony of informants. They often used the testimony of children to incarcerate their own parents. Friends and family of particularly wealthy Romans were coerced into making statements that would result in incarceration and the confiscation of much of the wealth of the Roman world. The Christians even stooped to the use of physical torture—which they even performed on children—in order to obtain confessions that could be used to obtain the property of unfortunate pagan suspects.

The earliest anti-drug legislation was not passed overnight. It took approximately two hundred years to pass such draconian measures. The first drug laws were meant to discourage drug use in the general population of sacramental users—that is, drugs used in religious rituals. Eventually, laws were written to prohibit the use of specific drugs. And finally, as the populace at large began accepting the stigma of drug use, all drugs were made illegal.

Christians argued that drugs were the tools of the devil; they taught that Lucifer was an active concocter of drugs and was present at any pagan rituals where drugs were used as a part of the ceremonies. The Christians declared the religious ecstasy of pagan celebrations to be a form of demon possession. In the end, the anti-drug laws were even extended to the use of pharmaceuticals by female physicians in the exercise of gynecology and obstetrics. That is, women's medicine became an important front in the earliest attempt by Christian bishops to obtain power in Rome.

The key to moving from simple laws that discouraged drug use to the strict laws of complete prohibition was the criminalization of the drug user himself. If pagans could be branded as "immoral" on the basis of their use of drugs in religious ceremonies, then the Christians could remove them from political offices and fill their vacancies with "moral" Christians.

Drugs Were Everywhere

In the centuries that led up to the rise of Christianity, drug users came from all segments of society. From the emperor himself to the most modest slave, drugs and drug use were ubiquitous elements of classical

BASILICA IN RAVENNA

> Nothing is more destructive for the soul than pure pleasure.
> —CLEMENT OF ALEXANDRIA
> EXHORTATION TO THE GREEKS

civilization. Opiates were commonplace remedies for pain, and potent narcotics made from opium poppies could be purchased at any open market in Rome, Greece, and Egypt. Plant extracts were used by physicians to treat many forms of disease—plants that could be easily purchased by non-physicians. Women regularly used psychoactive botanicals and animal-derived toxins to control their own menstruation; abortifacients were universally found in the drug stalls that dotted the landscape of ancient markets. Like recreational drug use, abortions were never legislated out of existence by emperors or even tyrants. The classical world that created democracy and the scientific method never banned the use of drugs or the performance of abortions—it simply refused to create legislation that governed the private lives of its citizens.

How exactly did drug use run afoul of Christians—who would themselves have been bound to rely on the same drugs for medical treatment? The answer lies in views of women's medicine and recreational drug use.

Mystery cults held immense power in the minds of common pagans. These religions regularly employed drugs in the form of compound incense in the performance of their rituals. People initiated into the mysteries typically imbibed or inhaled strong psychotropic botanicals at some time during the rites. These substances facilitated their communion with the cult statues of their gods and the visions they inspired. However, the drugs used in these ceremonies had developed from centuries of medical practice within colleges of female physicians. These women were considered the source and developers of these potent psychogenic substances.

As Christianity rose to prominence, it found itself in direct competition with popular mystery cults like those of Bacchus, Isis and Aphrodite. The quickest solution for the Christian priesthood was to vilify the one element that was common among the mysteries, yet was absent in Christianity—and it found this element in the use of mind-altering drugs.

Because the origin of pagan drug use rested firmly in medical traditions supported by women, the Christian hierarchy understood that limiting pagan drug use required actively targeting women's health—as it was practiced by the Romans and Greeks. Outlawing the use of drugs in religious practices alone would not limit pagan power unless the source of drug use could itself be targeted. Therefore, Christian priests, bishops and monks began an active campaign against female physicians, midwives and women who collected and sold drugs.

Of course, laws against the use of drugs crafted by the Church directly supported the notion that the elimination of pagan cult ritual was ostensibly an issue concerned with protecting children from demonic influence.

When Christian priests sodomized young boys, they rendered their victims inaccessible to pagan demons. Sexually violated children could not serve as hosts for pagan oracular gods; eliminating drug use by non-Christian cults was sold as just another measure taken by the Church to ensure the spiritual safety of anyone who might be tempted to get involved in pagan cults. That is, ritual sodomy and anti-drug decrees were simply two sides of the same social coin; whatever the true goal, both preserved an environment of support for the unrestrained abuse of children.

Chapter 10

Shattering an Old Paradigm

Christian priests considered classical myth to be as much an enemy of the Church as actual pagan cult practices. Stories of gods and goddesses transmitted pagan cultural values that ran contrary to Christian dogma, and the popular heroes and divinities of the Greeks and Romans were persecuted as intensely as the pagan priests and priestesses who burnt incense in celebration of their deities.

Some priestly offices—like that of the oracles—were closely connected with representations of divinities in ancient myth. Christian efforts to restructure classical culture ran especially afoul of the oracles and their ancillary priestesses. Specific temple guardians assigned to assist oracles presented a striking obstacle to the triumph of the Christian agenda. The oracles are among the first pagans attacked by the earliest Christians, as for example by Clement of Alexandria in his *Exhortation to the Greeks*.

Members of the Christian clergy, who designed, fostered and defended the rape of children, were attacked by pagans who upheld the pagan values of the Erinyes, an ancient offshoot of oracular servants who enforced primitive familial justice. Understanding the specifics of what the Erinyes symbolized sheds light on the motives of priests who held them in particular disdain.

> These practices must be eradicated, Most Holy Emperors, utterly eradicated and abolished. All must be set aright by the severest laws of your edicts...we know what punishments are appropriate for delusion.
>
> —FIRMICUS MATERNUS
> ON ROOTING OUT PAGANISM

FURIES AND ORESTES

The archaic Greek world feared the cult bodyguards known collectively as the "Wolves" and the "Dragons," but no group of women was ever more dreaded than the Erinyes. Like other Medusae charged with the protection of priestesses, the Erinyes ensured the safety of oracles while rigorously enforcing their pronouncements. When a tyrant had to be killed in order to protect the masses, the Erinyes applied the appropriate pressure to the local citizen population where he ruled. When wars had to be encouraged or discouraged, the Erinyes used their office to force the hands of local potentates. The Erinyes were masters of violence and intrigue, and their fierce loyalty to oracular cults was the result of an unbreakable chemical bond.

They were called Erinyes or "Furies" in Greek, but their office was much older than Hellenic civilization. The origins of the Furies lie in Persia, Mesopotamia and Egypt. These secretive oracular bodyguards were first called "Sphinxes." Their members were the female demons of myth, known for their half-human, half-animal forms. They were typically winged and possessed deadly powers. They may have possessed slight variations in their ancient artistic representations, but they were equally feared throughout the Near Eastern and Mediterranean worlds.

The Furies didn't merely pursue the guilty; they extended their justice to entire communities. When someone killed his or her own children or siblings or parents, the Furies were charged with punishing the entire community until the guilty parties, and any associated with them, were executed or exiled; the Furies, as dreaded Sphinxes, purged the stain of familial blood guilt from entire cities, and thus preserved the remaining members of the community.

Sphinxes went so far as to wage open war on individual city-states, under the authority of prominent oracular temples. As the representatives of the gods on earth, the Furies had complete authority and legal immunity to demand and carry out harsh forms of punishment for crimes against the natural bonds of the family. The Furies punished entire communities for crimes committed by their citizens—murder, greed, and a basic lack of common decency. These Medusae viewed crimes against family members as violations of the very core of nature. As a result, they considered offenses committed against family members to be a form of spiritual pollution—or miasma—and based their punishment on the principle that such a stain would affect the entire community until it was completely and irrevocably removed. The early Greeks believed that the world was populated by an "iron generation" of humans, who were afflicted with the incurable disease of greed; and they believed this greed naturally led to acts of betrayal and murder within the family unit itself. The Furies were meant to be a stabilizing force that would combat the natural greed of human civilization.

Who were the Furies? Who made up the ranks of the Sphinxes? According to the poets who wrote about them, they were the daughters of Night. They were originally primordial goddesses, whose charge was the protection of natural order. The Erinyes held the world together. Before the reign of Zeus, and the justice of the post-agricultural world, the Erinyes guaranteed the safety of the family unit—from its own potentially dangerous members.

Plays by Aeschylus

The Furies were made famous by Aeschylus, the Greek playwright who cultivated the performance of staged tragedies. Aeschylus wrote a series of plays about the ancient hero Orestes. In order to avenge the death of his father, Agamemnon, Orestes murdered his own mother in cold blood. He was commanded to do so by the oracular priestess of Delphi, who was well aware of the fact that his mother and her lover were responsible for Agamemnon's death. In other words, a teenage priestess ordered a prince to kill his own mother in order to avenge the murder of his father.

Although the crime of killing one's mother was viewed as a horrendous deed in the ancient world, Orestes can be excused because he was following Apollo when he decided to obey the oracular priestess at Delphi. Despite this, the Medusae known as the Erinyes were immediately dispatched to punish this obvious familial crime spree.

Orestes' greatest fear, despite the fact that he held the endorsement of the members of the religious community who worshipped the Olympians, was that he would be forced to face an ancient form of justice meted out by the Sphinxes—regardless of the endorsement of the priestess at Delphi. Under the command of the Delphic oracle, he thus fled to Athens, a city known for its support of Olympian justice.

According to Aeschylus, the Furies were able to drive the guilty insane. These Sphinxes possessed the power to summon the souls of murdered humans from the underworld, and then to send them to punish the guilty. In ancient Greece, when murderers began having nightmares about their victims, and started seeing visions of them in the night, it was said that the Furies were responsible. The psychological trauma of bloodshed inspired by greed or malice was the first sign of the presence of the Furies, and was meant to drive the murderer to the point of suicide. This madness even extended to the cruel murder of

MEDUSA,
EVELYN DE MORGAN

civilians by soldiers, who were known in antiquity to bear the psychological scars of their murderous acts.

> You have quaffed the virus of deadly poison, and under the stimulus of guilty frenzy you taste the cup of doom. The sequel of that food is always death and punishment.
> —FIRMICUS MATERNUS ON PAGAN INITIATION MYSTERIES USING DRUGS

The justice of the Furies predates that of the Classical Greek city-state. Aeschylus' Furies were indeed maniacal, but they were the guardians of a form of social justice that harkened back to the foundations of western culture. They drove Orestes insane, and sent him running into the arms of the Olympian gods in Athens—the same gods who established the modern court system—but their form of familial justice was met with respect.

The Furies, like all ancient Medusae, were associated with specific temples and their oracular priestesses. Furies, Wolves and Dragons were typically women—not just any women, but specifically teenage girls. Like the oracular priestesses they protected, the Medusae were chosen on the basis of distinct physical and mental characteristics and underwent rigorous initiation rites and training.

Childhood Bond

Other Medusae like the Furies all shared a unique childhood bond. Only girls who had undergone a specific childhood initiation known as "passing the child through the fire" were considered eligible to serve a temple priestess.

Soon after birth, select infants were handed over to special nurses, who were themselves members of the Medusae. These women subjected their charges to a two-fold chemical barrage. First, the Medusae performed daily purification rituals in which they burned potent botanicals in confined spaces and exposed their infants to the fumes for prolonged periods of time. Second, the nursing Medusae provided the infants with their own breast milk, which contained the mammary gland modified metabolites of a complex concoction of botanicals and snake toxins that they ingested on a daily basis.

Exposing infants to toxic fumes and breast milk containing snake venom resulted in numerous well-attested physical and mental changes that supposedly prepared the young for future priestly duties. As presented in our surviving myths, like that of Demeter and the child Demophoon, this chemical modification of infants was a painful and horrific process to observe—and was not for the faint of heart. However cruel it may have been, the young girls who endured these forms of ritual initiation were considered to have distinct advantages over the rest of their peers, and oftentimes became the oracular priestesses who set judicial and political policy in Greece.

The chemicals found in snake toxins have wide-ranging biological activities. For example, many venoms possess an affinity for activating the same receptors as prolactin, the human hormone responsible for the initiation of lactation following delivery. It makes perfect sense that these priestesses were able to nurse offspring without ever having given birth themselves.

In addition, many of the toxins found in snake venom are capable of modifying the metabolic activity of specific cells. The Greeks insisted that their Medusae possessed modified skin cells that resembled those of certain reptiles. The Medusae were known to possess the thick, hardened, scale-like skin of snakes, and ancient authors even speak of the mottled patterns of pigmentation found on their skin that mimicked the patterns of spotted snakes.

With snake venoms producing analgesics far more potent than botanically derived opiates like morphine, it is likely that the Medusae who ingested these poisons were indeed more resistant to pain and injury, as our ancient writers claimed. Hesiod, in the *Shield of Heracles*, addresses the superhuman abilities of the Erinyes and various snake-associated deities. In some extreme cases, the Greeks and Romans even claimed that these girls—the Medusae—developed their own poison glands after prolonged exposure to venom.

The symbol of the Medusae, in the form of the Sphinxes, the Dragons or the Erinyes, was an affront to the Christian fathers, who struggled to break the political and judicial authority of women. The Erinyes may have protected the ancient family from crime, but with the rise of the male-only Christian priesthood, they were completely wiped out.

Toppling Greek and Roman priestesses from positions of authority didn't just restrict the female political voice in antiquity; it placed a tangible limit upon the protection of children and the prevention of abuse. Roman critics of the Christians claimed for many years that priests preyed upon young orphans, who had no social mechanism for defense. When priests removed children from the streets and enrolled them in their services, the young kids had no legal recourse—and most importantly, there was no overriding religious protection of any crimes that might be committed against them.

Before Christianity gained authority as a state-sanctioned religion under Constantine and later emperors, women oracular priestesses could legally promote the protection of children; after the Christians gained the ability to manipulate imperial policy, the oracles disappeared, and young street kids became completely vulnerable. When the feminine authority of the "Furies" of Greek and Roman myth disappeared from society, culturally generated outrage for crimes against children was successfully stifled. The pagan condemnation of the child abuse of priests fell on deaf ears.

Chapter 11

A Monk by Any Other Name....

The Christian monk came to the fore on the stage of history when cultural customs concerned with the protection of children became the purview of men—and not just any men, but men of the cloth. This transference of traditional roles facilitated a much greater tolerance for child abuse within the Church. The teachings of monks are a reflection of both a virulent hatred of feminine authority and a disregard for the safety of children. The inflexible misogyny of Christian monks helped to create an environment that enabled priests to abuse children.

Christian monks didn't materialize out of thin air; they stepped into a vacuum left by Roman religious officials who followed in the footsteps of the earliest Greek temple servants who had protected priestesses and reinforced their proclamations. Archaic Greek Medusae defended and upheld the decrees of temple priestesses and thereby set a precedent for the generations of Greeks and Romans that followed. Christian monks merely assumed the roles that classical "enforcers" had carried out for centuries.

MEDUSA, DAVINCI

The Medusae who served oracular priestesses acted as the law enforcement, secret service and special operations agents of ancient temples; they carried out the will of the gods, as revealed by the priestesses they were sworn to protect. The Christian world had sim-

> What can I do? My mind is always thinking about fornication and does not let me rest even for an hour, and my heart is suffering.
>
> —QUESTION POSED TO A MONK

ilar sorts of religious figures, who attempted to live up to the highest and most extreme spiritual standards of "The Way." During the early history of the Church, Christian monks served Christianity in much the same way as the Sphinxes and Wolves served the Greco-Roman gods.

The Medusae were best known for their hatred of injustice. As temple guardians, these women enforced the declarations of oracular priestesses who were very much involved in civic affairs. It's fair to say the Medusae were wrapped up in human affairs.

When it came to ideology, Christian monks were very much the opposite of the Medusae. Rather than being burdened with earthly affairs, monks moved out of large urban centers into isolated communities where they prepared for the cataclysmic return of their messiah. Christian monks did not champion causes to further civilization. On the contrary, they promoted an ascetic lifestyle—and perhaps most symbolically important, they encouraged combat with the forces of spiritual darkness.

Like pagan Medusae, Christian monks possessed a distinctly independent authority. While they were indeed under the authority of the priestly hierarchy of the Church, they were much freer than priests and parishioners to set their own lifestyle and personal standards. In addition, monks, like oracular guardians, were considered to be the defenders of the ancient world's prophetic voice. This office gave them a level of respect not accorded to other religious figures. Monks, as the practical defenders of the Christian faith, had a way of communing with God that went beyond the forms of divine communication used by priests and Church elders.

The teachings of monks and hermits often provide an interesting glimpse into the psyche of the most involved and dedicated of the early Christians. Their thoughts and reflections tell us much about the undercurrent of opinion and ideology that flowed beneath the surface of official Church doctrine.

One particular story, the popular account of the life of a nameless hermit in Egypt, strikes a serious chord when considered against the background of the prominence of the feminine political voice in classical society and the stark contrast of the movement against women waged by priests in the first few centuries of the Common Era.

Extremist Monks

The monks of the early Church period sometimes carried the teachings of the Church fathers to an extreme, and frequently manifested the concretely bizarre expressions of theological theories and propositions demanded by Church officials. The story survives of one such monk in Egypt who struggled against the temptation to have intercourse by developing his own unique method of self-mutilation.

This hermit lived by himself and established his own reputation for continence, something highly valued in the community of ancient Christian monks, who, like most Church fathers, considered sexual intercourse with a woman to be a contaminating influence that always resulted in eternal judgment. At some point in this hermit's life, a woman familiar with the monk's sterling reputation made a wager with some local boys that she could successfully seduce him. The boys agreed to pay her if she could do so.

MONK

> Look what the child of the devil has done to me.
>
> —CHRISTIAN MONK ON LUST

After dark, the bet was on, and the presumably attractive woman approached the monk's domicile with ill intentions. After pretending to be lost and afraid, the girl pleaded with him to allow her to stay for the evening. The monk was visibly distressed by the proposition of keeping a young woman in his home for the evening, but he allowed her to stay in order to provide her charitable shelter.

As she predicted, it didn't take long for the monk to become aroused. However, his reaction to her feminine allure was not what she anticipated. For the monk became so preoccupied with his current sexual temptation and the prospect that he could end up in Hell if he should act on his impulses that he placed one of his fingers in the flame of an oil lamp. The monk stoically blackened his entire finger, to the point that it would be permanently deformed. This overwhelmed the girl with fright, and she cowered in the corner as the monk celebrated his willingness to sacrifice his physical well-being in order to maintain his continence.

The next morning, the boys who made the bet with the woman gathered outside the monk's dwelling, knowing that she had spent the night with him; they doubtlessly wanted to mock the poor monk for having given in to the temptation to have intercourse with the girl, and stood ready to celebrate her triumph.

Eventually, the door opened and the monk emerged with his hands tucked into his robes. The boys asked if a woman had spent the night with the monk, and the hermit replied in the affirmative and pointed them to the inside of the dwelling after telling them she was asleep. When the young men entered the home, they found the girl dead. Exiting the house in horror, they confronted the monk again. The proud, historically anonymous, ascetic monk removed his hands from his cloak and showed the stunned boys that every finger on his hands had been burnt to the bone. With an air of triumph, he proclaimed that the woman, a child of the devil, had cost him all his fingers.

The story of this nameless desert-dwelling monk's victory over the desires of the flesh was a tale related by Christians that was meant to illustrate the power of God and the ability of the followers of Christ to resist the onslaught of the devil. Christians spread the story of the Egyptian hermit who burned off all his fingers, not to express the horror and extremes of their beliefs, but to provide a positive example for all men, everywhere, who struggled with sexual temptation.

The ghastly reckoning of the story must have rattled even the Christian community, for the form of the tale handed down to posterity—as Desert Fathers, *On Lust*—includes an addendum that the monk raised the girl from the dead after the boys had learned their shocking lesson.

The story of this monk resonates with the myths surrounding the exploits of the Medusae who served oracular priestesses throughout the classical world. Christian monks, like temple bodyguards, were willing to go to extreme lengths to protect the dictates of their religious authorities—be they bishops, priests or simply New Testament scriptures. And like the Medusae, Christian monks perceived that they were at war with an element of their society that rejected their teachings.

Sources of Authority

Although pagan temples viewed their war as one waged with murderers, tyrants and the immensely wealthy aristocrats who trampled on the freedoms of the common person, Christian monks battled for the teachings of their own priests, regardless of their conception of justice and injustice. That is, the real differences between the monks and the religious pagans was simply the source of their authority: whereas the pagans believed their ultimate moral source was Nature, the Christians believed they were compelled to obey the dictates of the Church.

This difference is important when we consider the accomplishments of both groups and the stark contrast of their respective influences on western civilization. For example, the oracular temples and the Medusae who served them ultimately pushed the Greek world toward the creation of democracy. By intimidating and occasionally executing tyrants, the pagan religious world reinforced a natural democratic inclination. Much the opposite, Christian monks propped up and defended a political system that favored oppression and the subservience of all people to the will of a small oligarchy.

Christian monks were the "boots on the ground" of the cultural war between Christians and pagans. Monks put the teachings of priests into practice and essentially enforced the social demands of the Church. Monks taught that women were spiritually corrupt temptresses, whose allure was the work of demonic forces. And according to these same monks, all such trouble started with a young man's interest in a woman.

Monks abolished the figure of the nurturing woman who traditionally protected her offspring from masculine forms of abuse, and replaced her with a masculine defender of doctrine. The result was a cultural catastrophe, and the fear of judicial retribution by priests for crimes committed against children practically disappeared—as witnessed by the flippant attitude toward the victimization of children seen in the writings of such prominent Church fathers and abusers as Cyril and Ambrose.

This seeming disregard for human suffering shown by Christian priests and bishops was not just a personality flaw of callous individuals; it had very real consequences. Women and children became the victims of abuse and even murder, as a direct result. Despite pagan claims that the

> We cannot make temptations vanish, but we can struggle against them.
>
> —A MONK'S WORDS ON TEMPTATIONS OF THE FLESH

early Church was involved in various forms of sexual perversion, Church leaders continued to protect their own members; when monks attacked women for their sexual allure, they helped to redefine womanhood itself.

Chapter 12

Redefining Women

Christians didn't just denigrate and dominate women; they redefined them. Christian Zealots brutally and publicly murdered prominent and educated women like Hypatia, after branding them as "witches," or followers of Lucifer, but their efforts to control the feminine world also included a brilliant, behind-the-scenes reshaping of the western mind.

It's only logical that Christian priests redefined the roles of women. At the heart of their catechistic efforts to create subservient Church members by means of sexual abuse, priests had been forced to redefine themselves and their own roles as sexual purifiers. As sexual saviors, they divided the natural roles of masculinity and femininity by declaring them good or evil.

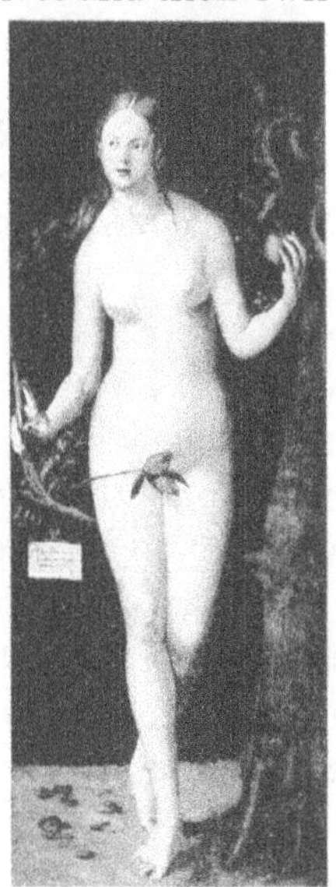

EVE, DURER

Priests even claimed that they were performing the work of "angels," the minsters of Jesus himself, by raping boys. Their masculine sexuality became an archetype of perfection and righteousness. In order to justify their own violent practices, they were required to vilify feminine sexuality, and thus redefine women in general.

In the early Christian centuries, the question of womanhood took center stage. Under the direction of monks, priests and bishops, the ancient conception of femininity was forever altered from its pagan base; over a period of four hundred years, women were systematically removed from political, religious, medical, and educational positions. And these women were replaced exclusively with Christian men. This gender transition heralded the destruction of democratic values in the ancient world and a marked turn toward tyranny. From the standpoint of the historian who studies the transition from classical to Christian civilization, it is fair to say that "as goes the woman, so goes society."

When the Christian religion redefined classical concepts like womanhood and femininity, it did so with the intent of uprooting the basis of pagan politics. Until the early centuries of the Common Era, women played a central role in the formation of classical culture. Christianity—under the direction of a male-only priesthood—recognized, as did the whole of the Mediterranean world, that the feminine voice was an integral element of pagan religion, politics and society. Feminine authority was an obstacle to the masculine priesthood of the followers of Jesus.

In its attempt to undermine the political and social authority of women, Christianity attempted to redefine womanhood itself. Much to the chagrin of the power brokers in the Christian Church, the classical world publicly celebrated and worshiped the feminine voice. In response, the teachers and dogmatists of the Christian world actively undervalued, undermined, and intentionally prohibited the expression of the female voice. The sweeping cultural changes we see in the second, third and fourth centuries of the Common Era were not an accident; the movement toward the repression of women was an intentional step toward an active campaign meant to redefine womanhood. In less than four centuries, Christian elders, bishops, priests and monks successfully altered the very fabric of western civilization.

Women's Benevolence

Before Christian monks began teaching that women were cursed, the Greco-Roman world worshipped the benevolent power of the feminine voice. The Greeks and Romans taught that women were politically relevant; they believed that women possessed a unique, divinely inspired ability to create beauty. They believed the cosmos had endowed women with gifts that were entirely absent in their male counterparts. The pre-Christian Mediterranean world believed the feminine voice was uniquely powerful—they believed it was a reflection of the highest creative force of the universe. In the pagan mind, the creator was not a man, but a child-nourishing woman.

Ancient myth displays an innate and profound respect for the feminine voice as a practical and authoritative guide for lawful, human civilization. The Greeks and Romans believed that women had a capacity for a particular social insight—something that was unavailable to men. This power to nourish included, but was not limited to, a woman's ability to procreate. Pregnancy and birth were just one manifestation of the higher natural order in which women played a more dominant role than men. Stated simply, the Greeks and Romans followed a simple principle with respect to the sexes: Women are attuned to a natural harmony that grants them the ability to create; and as a result of this social respect, women of antiquity created music, philosophy, science and ultimately democracy.

The ancient world also believed that masculine beings were incapable of experiencing the cyclical patterns of the natural world that fostered the creative gifts of womanhood. Consequently, long before the rise of democracy in Athens, the archaic Greek world fostered the development of the feminine voice as a guardian of civil liberty.

The earliest western gods of creation were feminine; the earliest western art forms were depictions of feminine gods. It would be easy to speak of myths of generation—from all corners of the globe—that establish the superiority of

> These are not the teachings of a healthy mind.
> —PORPHYRY ON PAUL THE APOSTLE

the feminine voice as a guide for human society; the archaic veneration of the Muses, the adoration of oracles, and the dominance of the Sybil were the western world's earliest dependence on the female voice as the foundation of civilization.

The earliest expressions of the feminine voice—the first to be attacked by the male-only priesthood of the Christians—were the oracles. The oracles formed the backbone of the ancient political world. Their pronouncements, which came from temples situated throughout the Mediterranean, guided and fostered the development of western civilization and held more authority than any local king or potentate. In antiquity, male-only armies, with their male-only leadership, obtained moral and spiritual authority to undertake wars by obtaining permission from these oracles. When kings desired to found colonies and expand economically, they also required the nod of female oracles. The highest judicial decisions of antiquity were not handed down by male judges, but by the oracles themselves. The feminine voice superseded any decision in any male-dominated judicial system; when the oracle spoke, her words were the expression of the cosmos, and could never be ignored—even Alexander the Great required the blessings of the oracle at Delphi. Interestingly, the priestess refused to speak with him; he dragged her around by the hair until she gave an answer, but his premature death reinforced the ancient belief that the oracles must be respected.

After the rise of democracy in Athens, the oracles still maintained the highest judicial authority; their appeal was not to a masculine code of laws, but to the cosmic feminine voice. Christians as early as the apostles understood that the classical world's respect for the feminine voice had prevented a male priesthood from ever gaining total political authority. If the Christians were ever going to succeed in usurping political power, they would need to declare a cultural war against the centuries-old belief that the feminine voice was the highest moral and spiritual authority; and in fact, this is exactly what they did.

The earliest Christians, the generation that immediately followed Jesus, was the first to undermine the pagan views of womanhood. Paul the apostle was perhaps the most aggressive opponent of pagan feminine vision; he went so far as to ban women from expressing themselves in a public forum. Under Paul's leadership, the early Christians associated feminine religious piety with strict silence and unquestioning subservience to masculine leadership.

What was unique about Paul's approach was that for the first time in western history the feminine voice became associated with immorality. No form of expression was tolerated; a woman's beliefs and views were irrelevant and even dangerous, because her voice itself—in the Christian mind—was utterly and irredeemably corrupt due to its influence by demons.

The Evils of Women

The next logical step for the Christian world was to apply the spiritual concept of the corrupt feminine voice to the physical world; that is, if women's voices were tainted by evil, then so were their bodies. And that is indeed what the early Church fathers aggressively taught. The ideas, no matter how heinous and bigoted, mutually reinforced each other.

ATHENA

In the early Christian centuries, a woman's appearance, like her voice, became tainted with the stain of moral, spiritual, and political corruption. Priests and monks taught that women should be entirely covered in public. Sexual inactivity was praised as a virtue, and female allure became an object of derision and loathing. The early priesthood effortlessly cultivated a virulent hatred and anxiety for the political expression of women that was directly linked to their sexuality.

Classical women had been naked for centuries; the art that sprang up under the libertarian impetus of the Athenian democratic world avidly celebrated the naked feminine form. As a matter of fact, the earliest sporting events in Greece are likely to have been initiated by priestesses of Hera, who themselves performed their events in the nude—as did their later male counterparts in the Olympic Games.

Feminine beauty was celebrated by classical artists, philosophers and statesmen, but under Christianity, the female form—like the female political voice—became an expression of evil, and the art that followed this era betrays a distinct aversion to any hint at feminine expression. The war on sexuality under the Christian hierarchy was not a war on masculine sexuality; it was a war on everything feminine.

The patent fear and loathing for women found in the earliest Christian writings ultimately brought about the destruction of pagan religion and the downfall of the oracles. For example, St. Ambrose, in *On Virgins*, claims that in God's eyes women are lower than snakes. Jerome, another leader of the Catechesis, states in Letter 128 that young girls are death-dealing serpents who should only converse with their own gender. The female political voice was actively stifled by Christian priests who sought to overturn ancient customs that asserted the value of the feminine voice in the realms of politics, society and culture.

St. Jerome, a priest who lived at the peak of the Christian campaign against the feminine political voice, was an outspoken critic of women, individual liberty and even sexual intercourse. Jerome, in a work in which he confronts the problem of female sexuality, says that married men are slaves of the flesh and that sexually active men have been expelled, as was Adam, from a spiritual garden of paradise—namely virginity. He further proposes that heterosexual intercourse is a form of contamination.

And Jerome reveals an even greater malice toward young women. In the aforementioned work, this prominent priest and eventual saint of the Church claims that young, pretty, voluptuous girls are nothing more than "death dealing serpents." In a particularly disturbing section of the work, Jerome focuses all his ire on young women, and condemns them spiritually for their physical beauty; he even praises ugly women as the antidote to youthful beauty.

Jerome's attack on beauty is illustrative of the general Christian assault on the pagan veneration of the Kore—the teenage, blossoming girl.

St. Ambrose, the bishop of Milan, reinforced the spiritual teachings of Jerome that targeted women and female authority by claiming in his work *On Virgins* that women were rightfully slaves to men—and that God had thus established the natural order. Like Jerome, he teaches that sexual activity is a form of contamination.

While there are scores of Christian teachings that purposely denigrate the female political voice, it is important to realize that Christian propaganda aimed at women was unified and came from the highest ranks of the Church. Respected priests and bishops like Jerome and Ambrose taught together that women and sexuality were spiritually sullied and that men should live, work and rule without the influence of women.

Under the reign of Christian priests, bishops and emperors, female sexuality and the feminine political voice were considered forms of spiritual corruption, and the female religious figures and medical authorities who upheld the tenets of classical civilization were actively persecuted. As the western world turned away from a model of liberty and freedom, offered up by the feminine political voice, the Roman Empire wholeheartedly embraced tyranny. Political tyranny was intimately linked with the sexual abuse committed by priests. Both forms of tyranny sprang from the same source. When the Christian world denigrated women, it opened the doors for crimes against children.

Chapter 13

Christianity's Promotion of Pedophilia

Christianity redefined the ancient woman to the extent that it stripped her of age-old political and social rights. The priesthood's actions were neither accidental nor purposeless; redefining femininity reshaped society for both women and children.

The aggressive denigration of women and the association of feminine allure with spiritual corruption had one horrible consequence for western civilization: in taking a stance against the feminine voice, the Church willingly justified, promoted and defended pedophilia. The early Church purchased its political power at the expense of children and the women who protected them. Priests and bishops actively perpetuated the violent, institutional abuse and rape of young boys.

It's difficult to identify the most vitriolic of the Christian fathers, and perhaps even more difficult to distinguish them from ordinary priests and Church elders with more moderate misogynistic views. However, Tertullian, a late-second-century Christian, was certainly among the foremost authorities in antiquity to rigorously stigmatize and oppress women. His peculiar affinity for violent opposition to social and political rights for women set the stage for a centuries-long conflict with paganism that fostered the protection of pedophiles.

According to Tertullian, womankind—by means of women's tempting sexuality—had brought sin into the world, thus forcing the son of God, the most virtuous of men, to be put to death. According to Tertullian, Eve's greatest vice was her beauty; Eve's sexual allure was meant to

> When the depths of our hearts have been stripped of unclean thoughts, let them dream of you.
>
> —AMBROSE
> ON PASSIONS OF DESIRE

attract only the devil and thus allow evil to come into the world. In the eyes of Tertullian, femininity was a gateway for vice and ruin; it was certainly the duty of all Christian men—themselves sons of the sexually deceived first man—to oppose the perceived power of women.

Tertullian summed up his views of women in a single sentence. In an apologetic work meant to defend his religion, Tertullian said: "The Christian man, once saved, no longer sees women: he is blind to feminine allure." And with these words, Tertullian provided an entire generation of priest pedophiles with the theological justification for the rape of boys.

The real problem with the misogynistic rhetoric of the early Church, found in authors like Tertullian, was what appeared to the pagan world to be an attack directed against the goddess Venus. Venus was Desire—particularly feminine sexual attraction. Condemning any attraction to the female form was nothing less than a crime against Nature; it was a view in dissonance with the created world, and the pagans believed the Christians would suffer serious consequences for meddling with the natural makeup of the cosmos.

Tertullian, like Paul, Peter and Jesus, may have preferred to "cast out his eyes" rather than use them to "lust after a woman," but his public push to stifle any trace of feminine sexuality had dire, and readily observable, consequences.

Within a century after the death of Tertullian, violent and aggressive Christian movements meant to stifle female sexuality sprang up in Europe, Asia and Africa. Women were forced to wear non-revealing clothing; young girls and mature women were forbidden from using makeup—something the Romans had been quite fond of—and those who had the audacity to adorn their skin with pigments made from botanicals and animal products were labeled prostitutes. Women were stripped of their jewelry, and eventually limited in their ability to appear in public.

The dire consequences of Christian social movements designed to stifle female sexuality were manifold and arose from the basic sexual philosophy that the Christians had attempted to prohibit. Stated otherwise, these movements, by their very nature, supported the promotion of pedophilia.

According to the pagan world, Venus was the dominant sexual element of the cosmos; as a creator, she was depicted as a conveyor of attraction—something that made her role in the universe a very active one. The masculine desire to "celebrate Venus" was considered a response, a passive reaction to a desire initiated by the goddess. In other words, following Venus (aka "desire") meant answering a call given by a receptive female; the pagan world viewed this masculine response to female sexuality as a form of non-violent submission.

When Christianity condemned classical female sexual allurement as a tool of Lucifer, it simultaneously condemned the passivity of the male sexual response and promoted the role of the male aggressor—one who partakes actively in the sexual act by pacifying the object of his desire. Eve, like Venus, was considered to possess power by means of her force of attraction; Christian Church fathers labored to transfer the pagan concept of active, dominant sexuality from the feminine to the masculine sexual experience.

VENUS, DURER

In an attempt to quell the powers of feminine sexual attraction, the Christians created a serious social problem, which the pagans claimed was a conundrum of their own making. The Church spiritually criminalized the attraction of a man

> You are like the holy Church, which is unsullied by intercourse, fruitful in bearing, a virgin in chastity and a mother in offspring.
>
> —AMBROSE ON SEXUALITY

for a woman, but simultaneously demanded that the masculine sexual role be the dominant one. Thus, in the third and fourth centuries, for the first time in western history, sex became a tool of spiritual dominance; intercourse was viewed as a heavenly act, employed exclusively by men, in order to further the kingdom of god.

A Novel View of Sex

When this novel view of sex as a spiritually significant, masculine act was combined with the emerging Christian belief in the virtue of suffering and the value of temptation for the purification of the soul, the first institutional pedophiles were born. For decades, Christian priests had taught that their God used special trials of temptation to cleanse, test and initiate believers. Special priests known as "exorcists" believed that they could summon the devil himself, and that by way of possession, they could apply the "fires of temptation" to an initiate, in order to establish these new believers as members of the body of Christ. Otherwise stated, priests forced young candidates for baptism to confront sexual pleasure in the form of rape; in a dominant, masculine role, priests tempted young initiates with forced sexual acts, in order to encourage them to flee the sin and prove themselves as secure followers of Jesus.

> If a man is called with the marks of circumcision—that is, a virgin—'let him not become uncircumcised'—that is, let him not seek the coat of marriage given to Adam on his expulsion from the paradise of virginity.
>
> —JEROME ON SEXUALITY

By applying "the fires of temptation" to young initiates, the Christian priesthood was able to establish its own sexual dominance, while denying the precepts of competing pagan religions. Cults of Dionysus, Pan and Osiris may have been celebrated by the public with the display and veneration of large phallic objects—something the Christian clergy vehemently condemned—but each of the gods who represented a form of masculine sexuality was considered to be subservient to the feminine authority of Venus. By abolishing the pagan concept of sexual receptivity from the celebration of intercourse, the Christian priesthood established its own cult precedent: forced intercourse was a valid means of ritual purification. And with this, exorcist priests obtained the moral and ecclesiastical authority to sodomize initiates.

For centuries following the misogynistic pronouncements of authors like the Church father Tertullian, the pagans argued that the Christian attack on Venus was merely one aspect of an all-out war on sexuality; they believed unnatural views of human sexuality ultimately turned the most ardent Christians into sexual deviants—or perhaps in modern parlance, predators.

We know that the pagans considered the Christians sexually perverted because, despite the fact that Christian monks destroyed any documents critical of the clergy, the Christian fathers themselves wrote in great detail about the many ways they ran afoul of the non-Christian population.

Of course, Christianity eventually won the cultural war it initiated against the pagan world during the late Roman Empire, and the medieval period was born. The pagans claimed that the Christian cultural victory over their age-old traditions was made possible by the fear they instilled in their new members. This psychological weapon, a distinctive characteristic of early Christianity,

JUNO

> Where there is fear, there is observation of the commandments; where the commandments are observed, there is a cleansing of the flesh.
>
> —GREGORY OF NAZIANZUS ON THE EFFECTIVE USE OF FEAR

was reinforced by episodes of intense sexual abuse. Christian priests used fear and abuse as a means of converting the pagan masses to willing and subservient stewards of Christian authority.

As a result of their cultural victory, Christian culture came to dominate the retelling of classical history, and most historians, even of the modern era, have argued from the Christian perspective—particularly with respect to sexual matters. Contrary to the expected—and often recorded—historical accounts, Christianity did not enforce a higher moral sexual standard, but instead, it initiated a period of sexual brutality; the Church ushered in an age of abuse and rape.

The pagan warning against abandoning Nature for dogma went unheeded, and the age of the institutional pedophile was unleashed on western civilization. For the first time in western history, sexual predators were given state-sanctioned protection. No matter how much the non-Christian population protested, pedophiles remained insulated in the Church, where they could pursue their practices without any fear of justice.

Ritual rape within the Church was standardized within just a few centuries of the death of Christ. The consistent application of a standard means for abusing children is evidenced in the writings of the earliest leaders of the catechetical schools that sponsored the indoctrination of new members. However, these standards did not just reinforce prohibitions; they also employed a positive element in the spiritual lives of initiates. Priests used the concept of "inspiration," a religious idea that was universal in pagan culture, to provide positive reinforcement for the brutality of their sodomy ritual. The Church's Holy Spirit became a psychological and inspirational means of positively reinforcing altered views of sexual intercourse forced upon new members.

Chapter 14

Death of the Muses

In order to spread the faith of Christianity, priests had to discover a process whereby they could indoctrinate members of the Church in a way that would ensure future obedience and loyalty. Most importantly, they had to convert young men with an interest in female sexuality to a system of beliefs that declared the woman to be the source of all evil. The ritual sodomy of young boys was not an aimless event; priests, exorcists and bishops designed the ceremony as a means of inculcating new members in a "way" that would guarantee their adherence to Church social standards and future participation in Church-sanctioned events. Under their direction, sexual abuse became a potent means of cementing doctrine in the psyche of new members by reinforcing their teachings with physical and mental trauma.

"Catechism" is a late Greek term that is best translated literally by the Latin roots of the word "indoctrination." It is largely a word that was manufactured to describe the period of time in the life of the new Christian that preceded baptism and the first communion. Catechism was a lengthy and strenuous exercise, during which priests and elders focused on imparting basic Christian theology to young initiates in a way that would promote their personal salvation.

> But everything else should be driven far away: fornication, adultery, and every form of self-indulgence. Keep your body pure for the Lord, to make it fit for his eyes.
>
> —CYRIL
> CATECHESIS

An important element of early Christian catechism

was the public renunciation of sexual pleasure. It was during this portion of the Catholic initiation that priests presented sexual temptation to young boys in an attempt to purify them.

Catechism could not be successful without the aid of the third masculine member of the trinity, known as the "Holy Spirit." This sacred spirit of inspiration was very much the masculine counterpart of the pagan Muses. The Holy Spirit was the answer to the classical conundrum of the influence of art and poetry in the promotion of pagan values. Christianity replaced the Muses and their influence on the ancient world with the figure of the Holy Spirit.

This is important, because the catechist could only be successful if he could see the spiritual truths behind the physical reality of his rigorous and painful initiation. The character of the Holy Spirit is the exact reverse template of the Muses.

Who were the pagan Muses? The Muses were the only gods to stand with mortals. The pagans believed the Muses inspired certain people with a more complete understanding of the cosmos. They nourished mortals as a nursemaid would sustain a child. There were nine Muses, the daughters of Memory. Their cult is one of the oldest in Greece; it was nothing less than the foundation of all Greek culture.

The nine Muses were kourai, or teenagers. They were portrayed as young girls in the bloom of life. They were dancers who taught human beings through the wisdom of song and poetry.

The Orphics were an ancient Greek religious association whose members worshipped a son of the Muses known as Orpheus. They were dedicated to the cultivation of the Muses and were devout worshippers of Aphrodite and Dionysus. They also believed the Muses were able to create a fully developed human mind by means of their inspiration. They thought this inspiration gave poets, as the servants of the Muses, an ordered understanding of the cycle of life; on the other hand, they thought mortals who ignored the voice of inspiration were destined for oblivion.

> The most fortunate person alive is the one loved by the Muses.
> —HYMN TO THE MUSES

Greek and Roman poets spoke of the Muses as if they were tangible, visible, living entities. A Muse could inspire a poet, teach an astronomer, or give a dancer grace. Poets prayed to them to ask for guidance; many ancient performers even boasted of individual and very personal relationships with specific Muses. The poet's success was attributed to the divine guidance of the Muses, but without a Muse, talent was nothing.

The Muses were not the origin of truth—the Greeks and Romans never claimed to possess any sort of absolute truth or orthodoxy. The Muses were vehicles of inspiration; they were the source of revelation—specifically, they guided mortals into an understanding of the immortals.

Libraries and Universities

Ancient temples to the Muses dot the landscape of the modern Mediterranean. Long after the foundation of these holy sites, the temples to the Muses became the foundation for our modern libraries and universities. An ancient temple to the Muse was called a Museum. It was a place of worship, where the nine sisters inspired education and learning. The libraries of the ancient world, which contained the assembled works of Greek poets, were associated with the temples to the Muses.

MUSE CLIO

All the dances in the ancient world, all of the drama, every chorus, all public ritual itself hearkens back to the worship of the Muses. With the passage of time, each Muse became associated with a specific discipline. For example, Urania was the Muse of astronomy, Clio was the Muse of history, and Erato was the Muse of love poetry. Poets, historians, playwrights, epic poets, lyric poets and philosophers invoked the Muses. They publicly acknowledged the role of the gods of inspiration, and frequently dedicated the first lines of their poetry to them. In fact, many of the most prominent ancient authors claimed that they were given their material directly by the gods and that their talent was not of their own invention.

The concept of possession has its origins in the worship of the Muses. The ancient world believed the spirit of the Muses could possess an individual in a sort of ecstasy—and the Greeks called these possessive forces "demons," or "daimones" in Greek, which was just their word for "divine being." The Greeks described this form of possession as the breath of the Muses. Poets believed the daughters of Memory literally breathed their voice into the hearts and minds of poets; from this process, the west derives its concept of "inspiration."

The classical concept of "possession" originated with the Muses, whose sole purpose was to make clear, or publish, the actions of the immortal forces that controlled the universe. In this way the Muses symbolized the highest source of wisdom—a direct link between the natural world and the humans who inhabited it. The Muses were the voice of Nature.

Once the concept of possession became prevalent in the ancient world—the possession of the Muses—the concept of "theurgy" became a reality. Theurgy was the process whereby normal people could force themselves to be possessed by the gods. Pagans practiced theurgy by enabling religious worshippers to inhale or ingest psychotropic substances derived from plants and animals, within a cult context. In other words, classical priests and priestesses allowed religious celebrants to become intoxicated in the presence of cult statues, which were widely believed to become animated in the eyes of the acolyte.

Ancient priests and priestesses burned incense on altars in order to generate fumes that could facilitate a mantic state for the worshipper. The incense burning ritual was the reason cult statues were so prominent. The cult statue was not merely a work of art; it was actually a device whereby the cult could promote visual and auditory direction of the god worshipped. The pagans came to temples looking for some sort of communion with the gods; in response, priests provided a context in which these people could directly visualize and even converse with their particular god.

How did theurgy work? After a series of ritual purifications—that may have included bathing and extensive fasting—the local priest or priestess would make an incense offering of locally purchased psychotropic plants. The celebrant, sitting or standing within view of the cult statue, would breathe in the vapors of this offering and would then proceed to visualize the god.

The Statue Speaks

Ancient accounts of theurgy are as tantalizing as they are foreign to modern audiences. Those who participated in these performances were oftentimes thoroughly convinced that cult statues could open their eyes and make personal appeals to the celebrants. Even the Roman emperor Julian who ruled 361-363 C.E. was fascinated by theurgy. After participating in a ritual in which he swore the statue of the goddess spoke with him personally, the emperor decided to press his campaign to restore the ancient temples that the Christians had allowed to fall into disrepair. Julian and his fellow attendees, all of whom were educated Romans, were convinced that the cult statue had actually been animated and had spoken to them directly.

MUSE TERPSICHORE

It's especially striking that theurgy had so few ancient skeptics. The Egyptians, Greeks and Romans were thoroughly convinced that specialized priests and priestesses were fully capable of making statues of gods come

> My child, do not be filled with passion, for passion leads to sexual immorality...do not practice divination since this leads to idolatry.
>
> —DIDACHE ON THEURGY

to life and speak to the crowds. Much like the cult of Eleusis, which employed a form of LSD to enhance the visualization of the rising goddess Persephone, religious authorities from all over the Mediterranean were able to use plants and animal toxins to enable people to visualize their gods. Even the Christians were unable to refute that the pagans were able to animate statues. Instead of condemning these pagan priests as frauds, the Christians claimed that they were able to summon demons by means of sorcery.

The apostle Paul adamantly prohibited theurgical operations, and was among the first westerners to define the process of animating statues as "idolatry" and "sorcery." The Christians were never skeptical, but instead attacked pagan theurgy on the grounds that their divine forces, or demons, were under the dominion of Lucifer himself, and should therefore be avoided. When the Church fathers, along with Paul, prohibited the worship of idols, they did so on the basis that the pagan practice of theurgy was incredibly popular and widespread.

As the Christians prohibited theurgy, as a practice that ultimately sprang from the worship of the Muses, they were forced to postulate their own source of divine inspiration. From the first and second centuries of the Christian era, the concept of the "Holy Spirit" emerges as a reaction to theurgy. The Holy Spirit, like the Muses, was the ultimate voice of god; but unlike the Muses, the third person in the trinity did not inspire people to celebrate Nature, but Christian doctrine instead. The movement away from the celebration of the Muses was the beginning of the darkest period in western history. The Muses brought education, art and ultimately democracy to the west. Without them, education crumbled, democratic principles disappeared, art was censored, and tyranny flourished.

Christian priests who oversaw catechism—and hence the sexual abuse of initiates—needed to promote the idea that the trials of the catechist were the physical manifestation of a much deeper spiritual truth that could best be made obvious by the Holy Spirit. Exorcists, priests and bishops were the vehicles whereby the devil, demons and angels could apply the fires of sexual temptation. Priests didn't actually sodomize children...their bodies did, under the influence of evil forces.

The doctrines behind catechism were certainly an elaborate spiritual construct meant to justify and defend child rape, but the invention of the Holy Spirit as a lens through which the initiates could interpret the seemingly horrific activities they were forced to endure as spiritual necessities of purification—while not attributing them directly to the offending priests—was nothing less than brutal genius.

Christianity replaced the classical Muse with a spirit that would be used to justify extreme abuse. Instead of inspiring the poets, as did the pagan goddess, the Holy Spirit allowed young victims of abuse to see their attackers as saviors.

Chapter 15

To Think Like a Priest

The figure of the Holy Spirit became the means whereby Christian priests could ultimately justify their horrendous acts of child rape to their own victims. The Holy Spirit was very much a faith-driven "perspective" that allowed the believer to turn away from the literal interpretation of the world around him to the contradictory explanation offered by sodomizing priests.

Assuming the "perspective" of the Holy Spirit enabled rape victims to justify their own abuse and their status--not as victims--but as the "purified." The cultural lens of the Holy Spirit reproduced the vision of the world advanced by the same people who stood to profit the most from ritualistic rape--the priests themselves. Replacing the world of reality with a manufactured Christian "perspective" was a successful means of reprogramming sexual-assault victims to perceive the world as their abusers wished them to see it.

The Holy Spirit provided a perspective that enabled young believers to reject sexual temptation: "You hear that our fathers were under the cloud, the good cloud that cooled the fires of the fleshly passions, the good cloud that overshadows those whom the Holy Spirit visits," wrote St. Ambrose in *On the Mysteries*.

Some of the earliest Christian writings shed light on the use of symbolism and "perspective" as a means of replacing pagan values with those advocated by Church officials. These written works also shed light on the sexual agenda of the early Church priests and their peculiar interest in sodomy.

One of the most outspoken proponents of Christian virtue was a well-educated Roman lawyer named Prudentius. As someone born into the 4th century's cultural war, Prudentius understood that issues of sexuality and the role of women in society were the linchpins of the ongoing Christian attempt to assume majority control of the Roman government. In an attempt to allegorize the socio-political agenda of the Church, Prudentius composed a 915-line poem titled "The War for the Soul." What the poem lacks in artistic depth it makes up for in verbalizing the psychological justification of Church policies that ultimately resulted in the incarceration, torture and execution of countless women, as well as the ritual rape of young boys.

Prudentius' work, the *Psychomachia*, is a poetic description of a "perceived" spiritual battle between personified pagan vices and Christian virtues. The poetry falls far short of Prudentius' Latin models, authors like Vergil and Horace, but it does reveal much about the reasoning and psychology behind the declarations, teachings and writings of many contemporary Church fathers, priests and bishops. In fact, Prudentius provides a vivid and rare glimpse into the minds of the Christians who labored to stifle the influence of women in society and government.

Within the first fifty lines of the poem, Prudentius quickly establishes the main villain of all Christians--and indeed, in his mind, of all the world--namely, sexual desire. "Libido," the word for sexual arousal in Latin, enters the stage of Prudentius' work on the male psyche as the greatest enemy of mankind.

JAMES, DURER

> A brother who sees a sister should think nothing of her being a female and she should think nothing about his being male. When you do these things, he [Jesus] says, 'the kingdom of my Father will come.'
>
> —SECOND CLEMENT ON THE ILLS OF SEXUALITY

For the author, sexual desire is a maddening impulse that subjugates humanity in a form of carnal slavery. And, of course, Libido is portrayed as a woman; not just any kind of woman, but a rabid, frenzied fiend.

Prudentius uses terms relating to madness and slavery to describe sexual arousal for one simple reason: he is not creating a new analogy, but instead is using the classical description of sexual arousal as a springboard. Christianity, as a cult, was certainly a novel invention, but it was nonetheless bound by the cultural traditions within which it was born and developed. Prudentius didn't just borrow from the pagans; he borrowed ideas and then grafted them onto the novel idea of Christian "faith," or "dogma."

According to the pagan world, desire was a goddess--whom they knew as Venus. Non-Christians believed this cosmic force was able to make fools of the wise by enslaving them to their own passions. Of course, the pagans believed such maddening slavery was in fact a good thing; after all, desire is the mother of creation, and every good pagan knew that Venus was Mother Nature, the entity responsible for generating and nourishing all creatures in existence. Without Venus, there are no flowers; and without the flowers, there is no bloom in life. In this way, the pagans venerated the sexual drive as the most benevolent, creative and productive aspect of all the cosmos.

As seen in the *Psychomachia*, the Christians took this pagan form of nature worship, something that venerated Venus as the great creator goddess, and turned it completely on its head. In Prudentius' work, sexual desire, or "libido," is not Mother Nature but instead the queen of all evil vice. She leads poor men away from their pursuit of Christ and corrupts them with various and sundry temptations of the flesh.

Men as Victims

Prudentius presents men as particularly susceptible to the burning trials of Libido. In his eyes, the masculine gender is the special victim of the whims of this terrible vice known as sexual arousal.

When Prudentius presented men--as opposed to women--as the particular victims of sexual desire, he was not deviating in the least from other Christian authors. Paul the apostle famously said it was better never to marry, but better to marry than burn; in *I Corinthians* he even advised the Corinthians that a father who had raped his daughter, or possessed the desire to do so because she was "sexually ripe," should be allowed to marry her.

Along the same lines, Origen, a great Christian scholar, castrated himself in an attempt to uphold principles taught by Jesus, and in performing the rite attempted to cast off his offending member as his spiritual master had commanded. In fact, early Christian men who left books to posterity typically reflect a single unified understanding of the male as the sexual victim of female allure, and look on sex as an evil.

Prudentius' focus on men as the sexual victims of devil-inspired women is not unusual or particularly revealing. However, this Roman lawyer does give historians one incredibly valuable insight that seems far less patent in other Christian authors, despite the fact that it lingers under the surface of their works: He associates male sexual temptation with sodomy. In fact, Prudentius assigns to his main villain, the queen of all vice, a particularly interesting name; he calls her "Anal-intercourse Lust," or "Sodomita Libido" in Latin.

In other words, this Christian intellectual, who emerged from the century that produced the final victory of the male-exclusive Christian priesthood over the pagan oracular priestesses, considered the greatest temptation to be the act of anal intercourse. In fact, he graphically describes the power of such desires inherent in the Christian community of men, and demonstrates what appears at times to be incredible self-loathing---if not just a patent disgust for the fact that such desires can be found universally in the hearts of Christian men.

According to Prudentius, the lust for anal intercourse drives men to the gates of Hell, and even stains the body with a visible form of corruption. The language he uses to describe the taint of anal sex is so similar to that used by other Church fathers that it cannot escape the notice of historians that Prudentius was probably participating in a much broader dialogue on the act of sodomy. In fact, the question of sodomy, with its dark fires of temptation, surfaces repeatedly in the discussion of the proper initiation of young boys into the Church.

Prudentius does not stop with merely mentioning sodomy as the great temptress of mortal men. As his poem about the epic battle for man's soul continues, he narrates that Chastity conquers Lust in hand-to-hand combat; as a result of this metaphorical victory, the bodies of the followers of Jesus are cleansed forever from the stain of sodomy, and thus preserved for the private use of their master.

From Sodomy to Jesus

Stated otherwise, according to this celebrated Christian poet, true Christian men are ultimately cleansed of the stain of sodomy and handed over to Jesus--in order to give to their Lord exactly what they had been giving to the queen of Lust. The transference of one sexual partner for another is crystal clear in the original Latin text: "No longer

JESUS, DURER

tempt those who worship Christ, Libido, you most rabid monster, so that their bodies may remain undefiled for the use of their own king." In short, Prudentius proposed that the act of sodomy can be used to serve Christ rather than one's own selfish desires.

> On the other hand, wherever one finds a crowd of adolescent boys... there will the Christian teachers be also.
> —CELSUS
> ON THE HABITS OF PRIESTS

What is perhaps more telling than Prudentius' literary foray into the struggle of men to overcome their desire for sodomy is a later section of the Psychomachia that discusses the spiritual prize of young boys. Just about a third of the way through the poem, Prudentius composes a speech of victory for the Christian virtue "Hope." Her speech is a direct and obvious indictment of the pagan world. In her soliloquy, Hope praises the highest and most virtuous human relationship possible—that of Christ with a young boy.

In order to illustrate her point, Hope gives us the example of the young King David, who fought the monstrous Goliath. She describes David as a young boy, with toys, who was entering the ripening of his youth when he killed the giant. The Latin word for boy here describes a pre-pubertal youth and can even be translated as child. It's important to note that Prudentius was not referring to an adult male or even a pubescent adolescent; he was making a distinct reference to a young male child, who had not yet matured sexually.

Prudentius' character, Hope, speaks about the "flowering" of the young boy as a symbol of his great spiritual significance to Christ and his followers. It is clear from the text that the source of the boy's attractive qualities is his pre-sexual flowering. The use of this specific botanical vocabulary was meant to contrast with the pagan myths that spoke of the power of the blooming kore, who was herself a post-pubertal girl. It appears that Prudentius was transferring the idealized object of sexual desire from the pagan standard of a sexually developed girl to a novel Christian sexual ideal of an undeveloped boy.

The reference to the purity of young boys is not accidental. In fact, it flies in the face of the Greco-Roman portrayal of teenage girls as the highest form of oracular potential in the cosmos. In addition, asserting that young boys were the object of the affection of Jesus would tend to undercut or negate the authority of the many priestesses who served throughout the Mediterranean. In this way, Christians like Prudentius created a new paradigm for sexual desire while simultaneously undercutting the political authority of the pagan world.

Chapter 16

Mystery of the Lady-Boy

Christianity's reevaluation of sexual intercourse for the sake of political gain did not involve an interest in sodomy alone. Due to the exposure of early Christians to the figure of Hermaphroditus, the Greek god who possessed both masculine and feminine genitalia, some Church fathers explored the forbidden arena of the lady-boy, the curious man-woman of ancient myth whose special allure was responsible for his/her constant resurfacing in both European and Middle Eastern cultures.

And the same Christian priests who molested children found a way of adopting and adapting the pagan lady-boy for their own uses. This shadowy figure, who occasionally emerged in pagan mystery cults, ultimately ended up as a representative of Jesus himself. Once again, competing mystery religions forced the Christians to consider topics like hermaphroditism while at the same time encouraging them to adapt these ideas for their own purposes.

ST. JOHN
MICHELANGELO

Christianity's greatest rivals were the Roman, Greek and Egyptian mystery religions. Christianity came to power in competition with the followers of Aphrodite, Bacchus, Isis and Cybele. The Christians were adherents of a mystery religion, just as were their pagan contemporaries. In order to obtain and sustain the dedication of the non-Christian world, the followers of The Way grafted the familiar practices of pagan cults onto their own religion.

> The effeminate Liber [Dionysus] could not offer prolonged resistance to the united resolution of men. For it is common talk in the gymnasia of Greece that he was a pervert and served the lustful desires of homosexuals.
>
> —FIRMICUS MATERNUS ON DIONYSUS

The early Church first augmented its membership by converting the pagan followers of competing mystery religions. The cults of Aphrodite and Dionysus were among the most widespread and popular mystery religions of the 1st through the 4th centuries of the Common Era. Christianity successfully competed with the followers of mystery cults by denigrating them; in essence, the Christians undercut the legitimacy of competing mystery religions while adopting and adapting the very same practices.

Christian priests and bishops claimed victory over the followers of Aphrodite by declaring that the worship of the goddess was a conduit of "pornography." The same Christians attacked the followers of Dionysus by declaring ecstasy itself to be a sin—particularly drug-induced ecstasy. Both attacks were effective in turning public opinion against the pagan cults. In order to turn the cultural tide away from the pagan mysteries to their own, the Christians established their own moral high ground and claimed a superior ethic as the justification for the supremacy of their own mystery rites.

However, there was another popular mystery religion in Rome that the Christians were forced to deal with on an entirely different level. Mithraism was originally a Persian cult derived from the worship of Mithra, a savior-god of light. A Greek god, and

> Don't the people from Syracuse burn incense to Aphrodite "perfect ass," the same goddess the poet Nicander calls "she of the beautiful buns." I'm not even going to mention Dionysus the "pink pussy pounder."
>
> —CLEMENT OF ALEXANDRIA ON SEXUALITY AND PAGANISM

cousin of his Persian namesake, Mithras entered the classical pantheon of mystery cult gods and became a popular figure in the early centuries of the Common Era. The cult was particularly influential within the ranks of the Roman military; even emperors were initiated into its secretive rites. How did the Christian world compete? Christian priests didn't simply denigrate the worship of Mithras; they established a ceremony designed to directly counter its practices—something that would discredit the Mithraic cult while simultaneously attracting its discredited adherents to its own practices.

Importance of the Military

It is an incredibly important fact of history that Mithraism took hold in the Roman military. In the early centuries of the Christian era, soldiers actively cultivated the religion and spread it across the empire, leaving their subterranean cult complexes just about everywhere. This fact has great historical value, because the Roman military was a very effective means of spreading cultural values and social mores across the Mediterranean world. The Roman army wasn't just a tool for destruction; it was also an effective propaganda machine—something the Christians admittedly recognized.

Despite the widespread popularity of imperial Mithraism, Christians began aggressively populating the Roman military with their own adherents, and systematically uprooted the classical worship of Mithras, which they replaced with the worship of Jesus.

The best way to understand Roman imperial Mithraism is to examine its sacred iconography. The followers of Mithras met in underground chambers, many of which still lie beneath the foundations of Christian Churches across Europe today. In these underground vaults, which were constructed to facilitate some sort of initiatory offering and banquet, archeologists have found sacred images that contain a standard and highly reproduced theme. Scholars refer to this standard Mithraic image as the "tauroctony."

The different images of the tauroctony, pulled from underground chambers made by worshippers of Mithras throughout the Roman Empire, have a distinctly standardized iconography. Each depicts the slaying of a bull by the god Mithras; the god is depicted with his characteristic Phrygian cap, and is in some way stabbing the bull with a sword. Underneath the bull's wound, a dog and a serpent are typically portrayed lapping up the bull's blood. Finally, this image always includes the depiction of a scorpion, which is typically found somewhere near the testicles of the bull.

Classical scholars have argued for years about the best explanation of the tauroctony. It's variously understood that the figure of Mithras is involved in the ritual sacrifice of the bull, and it has been proposed that the animal figures represent astrological signs that would have been important to the worship of Mithras. Scholars believe the astrological symbols are a sort of map to understanding the influence of the zodiac on the practice of the cult. However, in the context of the religious activities of the followers of Mithras, there is a much simpler explanation of the symbols found in the tauroctony.

Priestly colleges, whose followers were designated as the servants of Draco and Lykaina (respectively the priestesses of the serpent and the wolf), held great influence in the practice of the mystery religions of the early Christian centuries. These priestesses originally formed the ranks of the "Medusae," the militant bodyguards of the Greek and Roman oracular priestesses who held such profound political power in the classical world. The snake and the dog in the Mithraic tauroctony are representatives of these two religious orders; the fact that they are drinking the bull's blood is indicative of the use of a specific drug in their own celebration of Mithras.

According to ancient medical authors, "bull's blood" was a highly toxic drug used to induce visions; the drug caused a frenzied mental state akin to some forms of temporary insanity. The orders of Draco and Lykaina believed the use of mind-altering drugs like this one facilitated their entrance into ecstatic trances, in which they could commune with the gods. In other words, the drug known euphemistically as "Bull's Blood" was a specific drug recipe used to facilitate communion with the Mithraic god.

Within the symbolism of the tauroctony, the snake, representing the order of Draco, and the wolf, representing the order of Lykaina, performed their duties as Medusae while under the influence of the drug known as "bull's blood." Nicander and Scribonius Largus, two ancient pagan pharmaceutical sources, both discuss the lethality of bull's blood and its effects on the mind. They also provide the proper antidotes for negative side effects that bull's blood could have on its users. In the image of the tauroctony, then, Mithras, the god of the cult, provides the drug to these Medusae as an instrument of protecting and growing the ancient mystery religions.

The presence of the scorpion in the tauroctony is fascinating, because of its obvious connection with the testicles of the bull; in fact, the scorpion sometimes appears to be aggressively attacking them. A look at ancient medical texts reveals that scorpion venom was a widespread pharmaceutical player in the world of cult drug use. It is likely that the scorpion's assault on the gonads of the Mithraic bull is simply a reflection of the use of this arachnid's venom by devotees of Mithras.

The mystery religions that thrived when the Church was in its infancy believed that the gods were attracted to mortals by the performance of specific activities; music, dramatic performances, drug intoxication, drunkenness and sexual ecstasy were all means of drawing certain gods from the ether of the spiritual world to the realm of mortal existence. For centuries, the Greeks used the phrase "going to Aphrodite" to represent sexual intercourse as the performance of an act that literally summoned the goddess.

The Greek god Mithras could also be drawn to the earth, or a human subject, in the same way that Dionysus could be attracted by inebriation, or Aphrodite by sex.

Like the followers of Cybele and Isis, the followers of Mithras appear to be involved in ornate and interesting sexual practices. The castration of the servants of mystery cults in the early empire is of no surprise to any historian or classical scholar. However, the means whereby the cult followers of Mithras achieved castration is biochemically elegant and reveals much about the ancient mystery religions with which Christianity was trying to compete.

Mithras and Sexuality

An interesting question for scholars concerns the gender of Mithras and the use of animal toxins to alter sexual identification. For example, Herodotus, the famous Greek historian of the 5th century, made a curious reference to Mithras in his discussion of Persia—-a statement that has troubled classicists for many years. In the first book of his *Histories*, Herodotus claimed that the god Mithras was known to the Greeks as Aphrodite-Urania. This is odd because Mithras is clearly a male god, and Aphrodite is the goddess of female sexual allure. Scholars may be confused by the reference, but the archaeology and the ancient literature bear out the accuracy of Herodotus. For example, Aphrodite is directly associated with gender-mixed deities, and she is the mother of Hermaphroditus, the ancient lady-boy. In addition, according to Hesiod in *Theogony*, Aphrodite was born from the "foam" of her father's castrated penis, when his children used a sickle to separate their parents, Earth and Sky. Scholars have even argued that a specific statue once identified as Aphrodite could not be the goddess because it is clearly a masculine figure—but this is only a problem of the modern world and did not trouble the pagans who actually participated in her cult.

It is important to note that Phanes, the paradigmatic lady-boy god, was associated with Mithras by the Orphics—the same religious cult that placed Aphrodite-Urania at the top of their pantheon, as the consort-sister god of Dionysus the gynomorph.

The image of the female god with a penis, or the lady-boy god, was an important aspect of the worship of each of the mystery cults that provided competition for the Christians of the second, third and fourth centuries. The lady-boy god played a part in the performance of the mysteries of Aphrodite, Dionysus, Cybele, Isis and Mithras. Christian elders knew, as did the pagans, that the mystery religions were actively employing scorpion venom, snake venom, and various botanicals to create pharmaceutical concoctions capable of altering human physiology along the lines of gender identification; they knew that specific cult drugs were capable of transforming boys into lady-boys.

The Christian world also knew that the pagan cults universally accepted the fact that a savior-god, like Mithras, could be drawn to the earth by means of specific bodily pleasures. In other words, in the Christian mind, if Mithras, like Phanes, was associated with sexual dimorphism, then the god would be naturally drawn to any sort of sexual activity performed by a lady-boy.

> Know the mysteries of love, and then you will be initiated into the lap [vagina/uterus] of the Father, whom God the once-born alone revealed. He is affection; and through affection He is known to us. The Father cannot be expressed, but the Mother shares an affinity with us. When the father showed affection, He became effeminate, and the proof of this is that He gave birth from himself.
>
> —CLEMENT
>
> THE RICH MAN'S SALVATION

And it is important to recognize that the Christians didn't believe the pagans were misled or delusional; in fact, the Christians taught that the pagan priestesses were worshipping actual demonic forces.

It should not be surprising then that the Christian hierarchy designed a specific ceremony meant to counter, or cast out, the Mithraic god, while at the same time summoning their own deity and thus perfecting the salvation of their initiates. In the end, the only way to conquer the demonic force known as Mithras or Aphrodite-Urania to the pagans was to summon him-her, and rebuke him-her in the name of the Jewish messiah. In other words, the only way to bring about the salvation of the young street kids who were taken into custody by the Christian Church was to force these children to reject the temptation offered by the pagan gods; and the only way to do this was to summon the demon-god himself, by performing a rite that placed these young, sexually undifferentiated boys in the sexual position of a receptive female with a penis.

In this way, the Christian priests of the early Church created their own lady-boys in order to further the kingdom of god and cast out the demonic forces of the pagan world. What was their justification for such an extreme act? They taught that Jesus was himself a lady-boy; the messiah was a man with breasts, uterus and penis.

Chapter 17

What Would Jesus Do With Breasts?

Why does St. Ambrose, the bishop of Milan, describe Jesus as having milky breasts and a uterus in *On Virgins*? For the very same reason that Jesus was arrested in the garden of Gethsemane with a naked young man, as reported in the gospel of Mark, 14:51-52. And undoubtedly for the same reason that early Christian priests claimed it was necessary to sodomize children. Because it was necessary for salvation.

As Christians of the early Common Era struggled to establish political legitimacy for themselves within the borders of the Roman Empire, they fought to redefine cultural values traditionally promoted by competing pagan religions. Over several centuries, Church fathers, priests, monks and bishops taught that sexual intercourse was an inherently evil act, and that women were the source of a taint of sin that permeated the universe and afflicted the male psyche. During this

JESUS IN THE GARDEN
EL GRECO

struggle to redefine sexual mores, Christian authors began publicly promoting their belief that pre-pubescent boys represented the purest form of human intimacy—and thus were the only rightful objects of sexual desire.

This shift from the pagan ideal of the post-pubertal female as the natural sexual partner of the adult male population to the pre-pubertal boy of Christian dogma was actively promoted by priests in a series of initiatory rites performed on new Christians. These rites culminated in ritual baptism, and novitiates were allowed to take communion as new members of the Church. Despite stiff resistance from the non-Christian population of the empire, the Christian hierarchy continued to foster and protect the priests responsible for carrying out initiation ceremonies that the pagan world considered criminal.

As Church authorities began successfully redefining social views of women and sexual intercourse, they gradually succeeded in limiting both the power and popularity of pagan mystery cults.

As popular and widespread traditional mystery cults lost ground to the Christian Church, they left a void that was eventually filled by their detractors. By the fourth and fifth centuries of the Common Era, the worship of Aphrodite, Dionysus, Cybele and Isis gave way to the pressure of the strict enforcement of anti-pagan laws instituted by Christians in the Roman government. The anti-drug, anti-homosexual, and anti-woman platform of the rising political power within the Church paved the way for the dismantling of long-established pagan mystery religions.

The disappearance of specific pagan cults and their age-old rites saddled Christianity with the responsibility of meeting the needs of the people who could no longer freely worship their native divinities. Christian leaders responded by absorbing the domains or purviews of the gods in question. For many of the ancient gods, this was not a problem. But with a few classical cults, particularly the mystery religions, the Christians were sometimes unsure of the best response to the demands and needs of their new members.

The cults of Aphrodite, Isis and Dionysus were dealt with by the Christians without serious damage to the consistency of their own religious dogma. Aphrodite and Isis were effectively erased from the social consciousness of the Mediterranean by the promotion of the idea that femininity could never be sacred, but was instead an irredeemable tool of the devil. In this way the Christians completely undercut the perceived value of both of these goddesses. In short, the cults of Aphrodite and Isis were rigorously prosecuted as illegal activities and their adherents were forced to go underground—or face imprisonment and/or execution. The moral laws of the Christians against sexuality and drug use enabled them to persecute and ultimately wipe out the followers of Aphrodite and Isis.

Dionysus and his cult following were absorbed rather than doctrinally deleted. In a quirk of history, the early Christians merely assimilated the phallic veneration of Bacchus. The ancient god's ecstasy-inducing wine was merely transformed into the Eucharist, and the worship of his erect penis became a ceremony known as "the cultivation of the founder's genitalia," which was celebrated as a secretive mystery.

In fact, much of the revelry that so characterized the pagan worship of Bacchus was directly transferred to nightly, secretive meetings of the Christian elect. Minucius Felix, a Roman Christian, reveals that members of the Church came together to celebrate or "cultivate" the erect phallus of their highest priest (Jesus), and reportedly participated in orgies that involved incestuous partnerships. In one particular ceremony, the Christians snuffed out the torches at a set point in their love feasts and, in the darkness, allowed Church members to

> Others say that they [the Christians] actually reverence the private parts of their director and high-priest, and adore his organs as parent of their being.
>
> —MINUCIUS FELIX
>
> ON THE MYSTERY OF THE ADORATION OF JESUS' PENIS

> They [the Christians] gather at a banquet with all their children, sisters, and mothers, people of either sex and every age. There, after full feasting, when the blood is heated and drink has inflamed the passions of incestuous lust... in the shameless dark lustful embraces are indiscriminately exchanged; and all alike, if not in act, yet by complicity, are involved in incest...
>
> —MINUCIUS FELIX ON REPORTS OF SECRETIVE CHRISTIAN PRACTICES

engage openly in anonymous intercourse. Contemporary pagans of the early centuries of the Common Era even claimed that the cult of "The Way" was involved in the consumption of dead or aborted fetuses—in what was obviously an adaptation of the sacred feasts of Dionysus. Christian priests absorbed the cult of Dionysus, rather than destroying it.

Takeover Tactics

The Christians assimilated the rites of Bacchus within their own cult practices, but the popular mystery cults of Mithras and Cybele, and the worship of the classical lady-boy god, demanded that the Christian priesthood employ a much higher level of sophistication when assuming the takeover of their ancient rites. After all, there was little precedent for a hermaphroditic divinity within the Jewish traditions, and the apostles and early Church fathers had not yet embraced such an idea.

For centuries before the rise of Christianity, the Mediterranean world participated in the spread of the mystery rites of Cybele. The goddess' Greek counterpart was Rhea, and her rites were advanced by a group of priests called the Galli, who ritually castrated themselves in honor of the goddess' lover, a man named Attis or Attes, who founded the mystery cult. According to the Greek author Lucian, this Attes was reportedly impotent, and dressed himself in women's clothing and spread religious rites involving a sort of hermaphroditic adulation of feminine power.

The rites of Cybele meshed well with the mystery cults of Aphrodite, Isis and Dionysus. The priestesses of Cybele were known to use drugs to enter ecstatic states from which they would publicly prophesy. Nicander, an author of all esoteric things-pharmaceutical, wrote about the oracles of Rhea, a group of girls who could be found in the highways and byways of the empire in a trance-like, drug-addled state, yelling aggressively at passersby.

For the Christians, the assimilation of the rites of Cybele presented a particularly difficult challenge. The adoption of the fervor of this popular cult required a true intellectual giant—and someone with tremendous political power. And in the late fourth century of the Common Era, as Christianity pounded nails into the cultural coffin of paganism, a figure of no less magnitude than the brilliant bishop of Milan, St. Ambrose, accepted the contest of assimilating the ancient cult of Cybele and adapting it to Christian theology.

How could Christianity find the justification to support a hermaphroditic savior? St. Ambrose masterfully drew from both the Old and New Testament authors to create the first official Christian Lady-Boy, the image of a messiah in the form of an emasculated, feminized and very sexually oriented Jesus.

In the first book of *On Virgins*, St. Ambrose spoke of a scriptural and prophetic, virginal Jesus, who had fully functional breasts and made himself the once-male, feminized partner of every believer. In this virgin allegory, St. Ambrose goes so far as to say that Jesus

JESUS, DURER

produces believers from his masculine womb, and feeds them with the milk of his breasts. In Ambrose's words, Jesus was the masculine "rock" that developed nourishing breasts in order to facilitate his role as the breast-feeding mother of the Church. In fact, Ambrose carries the point acerbically by ending his description of the feminized Jesus by claiming that it is perfectly natural that the son of god has his own teats.

A description of a man-god savior with female reproductive organs and breasts may be disturbing to a modern audience, but the pagan world, which at the time was still a large percentage of the population, would have quickly recognized their own hermaphroditic, nurturing divinities in the person of Jesus the virginal lady-boy.

Women Less Than Slaves

For Ambrose and the Christians of his generation, women were considered to be lower than slaves—something Ambrose claimed—and sexual intercourse with women was believed to be a contaminating process ultimately devised by the devil. Therefore, the prospect of sex with a virginal, sexually hermaphroditic boy was not only in step with the hugely popular cults of Cybele and Dionysus, but in a Christian theological sense it was perfectly pure and spiritually justifiable. In fact, the proposition of sex with the Jesus lady-boy also supported the assertions of generations of monks, priests and Church fathers who upheld the idea that a virginal, sexually undifferentiated, prepubertal child was the ideal sexual partner.

The Christian Church assimilated teachings and practices of pagan mystery religions that ultimately catapulted the cult of "The Way" from relative obscurity to complete and unfettered political dominance. As it gained political authority in the Roman Empire, Christian bishops and priests fostered and defended the ritual rape of young, pre-pubertal boys as a rite of initiation.

Christian priests raped young boys in Alexandria, Jerusalem and Rome for the very same reason. The Church wasn't a refuge for pedophiles; it was a place of indoctrination. Like Jesus in the Garden of Gethsemane, who was accompanied by a naked teenager, the Catholic clergy believed it was spreading the gospel by forcing young boys to come face to face with the renunciation of sexual pleasure. Priests forced prepubescent and pubescent boys to endure brutality-induced sexual pleasure while forcefully teaching them to renounce the desire for women and to embrace a renewed sexual purity they could obtain by rejecting the pleasures of forced intercourse.

Church fathers transformed the sexuality of Jesus, just as they altered perceptions of intercourse in the boys they abused. Ritual catechetical sodomy was an intense and effective means of indoctrinating young, inexperienced Christians while changing their views of sex. Priests manipulated prevailing sexual mores when they forced young converts to renounce the pleasures of male-female intercourse. The ritual was detailed, brutal, and consistent. Child rape was an institutional policy that embraced both Catholic theology and the Christian drive to transform the cultural makeup of the Roman Empire.

Chapter 18

The Child Rape Ritual Exposed

Early Christian priests altered perceptions of sexuality in Roman culture by employing child rape as a means of reinforcing indoctrination. Ancient child abuse within the Church was not the product of a few rogue pedophile priests; it was a deliberate, purposeful act, meant to change Roman perspectives on sexual intercourse and religion. The Christian hierarchy used the sexual assault of minors as a means of transforming a society steeped in the veneration of female sexual allure and feminine spiritual and political authority. The Christian war on classical values redefined morality and enabled priests to use extremely brutal mechanisms for changing the way people thought about sex.

All levels of the Christian hierarchy, including priests, exorcists and even bishops, advocated and defended the use of ritual sodomy. It appears that the ritual was most prominent in the catechetical school of Alexandria, and likely finds its origins there. It is also likely that the gospel writer Mark actually founded the catechetical school in Alexandria. Many Church leaders, including Clement, Origen and Jerome, were involved in its rigorous method of training of new converts.

Based on the writings of the early Church fathers, including prominent bishops, priests, intellectuals and even monks, it is possible to reconstruct much of the child sodomy ritual. Authors connected with catechetical schools yield a wealth of evidence that reveals ritual abuse to be a consistent, brutal, and highly effective means of indoctrination.

According to our ancient catechetical sources, if you were a Christian priest living in the earliest era of the Church, you knew what had to be done. Nothing was more merciful in the long run. Remove the masses of unfortunate, orphaned children from the streets, a few at a time, and prepare them for salvation; starve them, recite numerous creeds to them with a steady, droning, persistent repetition, and then gather them together into the secret chamber, a place that only priests were allowed to frequent. A place where the devil could be summoned; a place where a priest could forever purge them of their desire for sexual intimacy.

In may be hard for a modern audience to understand, but in the early centuries of the Common Era, salvation was no joke. Original Sin was a doctrine that non-Christians ignored—and even mocked—but exorcist priests took it very seriously and were specially trained to root it out.

Every good Christian knew that young boys, particularly orphaned children without the protection of living parents, were susceptible to sexual impurity—something that would drag their souls directly to Hell. The only way to purge this impulse, the only way to save their souls, was to force them to undergo a sacred ceremony, a mysterious initiation that would forever cleanse them of inappropriate sexual pleasure and deliver them to Christ.

Fires of Temptation

Contemporary Roman Christians knew of this ritual as applying "the fires of temptation." It was a devastatingly difficult indoctrination, meant to rescue the damned; it even required that a priest be on hand after its completion

THEATER EPIDAUROS

to fully debrief and counsel the shell-shocked initiates. The severity of Christian initiation disturbed the Romans, but in the eyes of the Church hierarchy, desperate spiritual times called for desperate spiritual measures.

Ritual exorcism is not difficult to comprehend. Its theology is as elegant as its rationale is unquestionable. In the mind of the Christian priest, the world is full of demons. And these demons have a peculiar affinity for naive, spiritually pure, pre-pubertal boys. Tertullian wrote in *Apologeticus* about the belief that Christians possessed a fiery breath that was able to send demons out of the bodies of the possessed; he says that demons flee the touch of Christians or their breath. This fits the historical context well when we consider that Cyril of Jerusalem, one of the greatest advocates of ritual sodomy, wrote in *Procatachesis* and *Mystagogical Catechesis* about the process of breathing or blowing upon young, nude, oiled boys: "Be earnest in submitting to the exorcisms. If you are blown upon and exorcised, the process brings you to salvation."

The battle for the soul revolved around the sexual encounter of these youths, and the Christians thought it could be won if the young were given a chance to renounce the devil—in the face of direct, unavoidable temptation. What better way to give sexually inexperienced children the opportunity to embrace salvation than to summon Lucifer himself? Let the Devil offer the pains of temptation, and then let the young reject him and flee to Jesus. The reasoning of the exorcist priests who ended up sodomizing boys was really that simple.

Post-ritual counseling was invaluable. After all, that's what Cyril, the bishop of Jerusalem, had commanded of his exorcist priests; that's what Clement, the head of the catechetical school in Alexandria, required of his students. And Church elders like Cyril and Clement were, after all, bearers of the divine commission. They were only a few generations removed from the Master himself; their authority was impeccable, and their dictates were obeyed because they were coming directly from God.

> You have swum into the Church's net. Allow yourself to be caught; don't try to escape. Jesus is fishing for you, not to kill you but to give you life once you have been killed.
>
> —CYRIL
> ON CHRISTIAN INITIATION

If you were a priest involved with catechesis, you were expected to teach children that forced intercourse is only a sin if it is enjoyed. The distinction between willful enjoyment of sodomy and forced enjoyment was critical to Cyril. After all, according to Christian dogma, if shunned, any sort of sexual activity became a means of purification. That is, the job of the exorcist was to summon the devil—let the prince of darkness offer the temptation through you, and then let the child reject the act. The successful initiate would be guaranteed salvation, and you, the priest, would be doing the work of Christ.

The ritual of purification by sodomy was carefully prescribed and executed. The catechetical schools insisted that the "mystery" remain consistent throughout the Empire. According to the bishop of Jerusalem, there must be an orthodox method of exorcism. This meant that exorcist priests were bound to follow the writings of the bishops and to allow local authorities to determine who was worthy of assisting in such sacred duties. St. Ambrose tells us that priests, elders and bishops were all present. But most importantly, priests and initiates were forbidden from discussing all the details of what happened during this sacred mystery—on pain of eternal damnation.

A Ritual of Abuse

Priests believed that only those who bore the onerous burden of summoning the devil himself and those who were successfully initiated could understand the value of ritual sexual abuse. All others should be excluded from knowledge of its specifics, wrote Cyril in *Procatechesis*: "Make sure that you don't talk carelessly, not because what you are told isn't fair to talk about, but because the listener isn't fit to hear it."

The Church fathers were well aware that the pagans would eventually accuse priests of crimes if they ever learned all the particulars of the initiation, precisely because they had not been born again into "The Way," and their natural inclination was to defend the demons they worshiped. In short, pagans were considered to be of the spirit of anti-Christ and not to be trusted with the secrets of initiation.

Young boys taken from the streets of large urban centers were prepared over a period of weeks for their catechesis. Priests enforced a rigorous series of fasts and constant indoctrination. This reinforced repetition of Christian doctrine was the reason the process came to be known as catechesis—which is just a Greek word for "placing doctrine into the ears" of novitiates; in Latin, "catechesis" is transliterated as "indoctrination."

After weeks of starvation and repetitive indoctrination, children deemed ready for the initiation ceremony were taken to an out-of-the-way chamber or location, where they were sequestered from the general population of novitiates. In the first step of the process of initiation, priests removed all of the clothing of these boys. If the children showed any evidence of being ashamed to stand before a group of priests naked, Cyril commanded that they be reminded that Jesus was himself crucified without his clothing; they had no need of embarrassment to stand as Jesus stood, naked before the world.

> For just as the breathing of the saints and the invocation of God burns like the fiercest flame and chases away the demons, so too the invocation of God together with prayer gives this exorcised oil such power that it can burn away the traces of sin and even repel the hidden powers of the evil one.
>
> —CYRIL
>
> ON THE POWERS OF EXORCISM OIL

> Satan is himself darkness and exerts his power in the dark.
>
> —CYRIL
> ON THE DEVIL

In Cyril's own words from his *Mystagogical Catechesis*: "As soon as you entered, you took off your tunic...Once you had taken it off you were naked...What a wonderful thing! You were naked in the eyes of all and felt no shame...Then, once you had removed your clothes, you were anointed with exorcised oil from the topmost hairs of your head to the lowest parts of your body."

After disrobing the children, the priests blindfolded them and then explained that their actions were a necessary step in protecting the children from the gaze of the devil. Next the priests rubbed the boys generously with a sacred oil. This sacred oil, like the anointing oils also used by the Christians, contained drugs that would undoubtedly facilitate the process of exposing the children to the temptation offered by Lucifer. In short, it would numb them to the burning fires of the devil.

Following Cyril's instructions, priests applied the holy oil to the boys, from the crown of their heads to the soles of their feet. It was an important priestly duty to ensure that the children were completely covered and that the holy oil was rubbed into the skin thoroughly. After all, it served as a barrier for their own protection, and once it was applied, the boys were forever consecrated to Christ. Cyril delights in this particular detail of the ritual and speaks about the necessity of rubbing the entire body with the oil.

Naked, Oiled Children

Once the children were prepped in this manner, and knelt in the hidden recesses of the Church, naked, blindfolded and covered with oil, the exorcist then proceeded to summon the devil. Once Lucifer had been summoned, he made his presence known to the initiates; they heard his voice, and became terribly afraid.

> Be earnest in submitting to the exorcisms. If you are blown upon and exorcised, the process brings you salvation... We are trying to get pure gold. Can the impurities be removed without fire?
>
> —CYRIL ON THE MYSTERIES OF FIRE

The boys were then commanded to rebuke the devil while facing him; then they were told to turn their back to him.

At this point, the possessed exorcist applied "the fires of temptation." Cyril forbade this knowledge from becoming public lest the pagan world misinterpret it and cause criminal trouble for priests. What we do know about the "fires of temptation" is that at least one Christian author reveals them as the act of sodomy. In other words, the prince of darkness, the author of the first temptation—while inhabiting the body of an exorcist—forced prepubescent boys to submit to anal intercourse. The devil was said to have done this in a violent manner, but the children were allowed to suffer the temptation forced on them by the possessed exorcist because this afforded them an opportunity to rebuke the pleasure of the sin, and thus obtain salvation.

The priests who were present during the application of "the fires of temptation" encouraged the children to flee the sexual advances of the devil and they were told that they should not enjoy the experience; the priests helped the children to call upon the name of the Lord—to see past the pain of temptation to the relief of salvation. When the devil was present, applying the sexual temptation, the boys were told to rebuke him in the name of Jesus; they rebuked his acts of violence, they rebuked his offer of carnal pleasure. Helping the children to renounce this forced sexual act allowed them to accept eternal salvation.

After the devil was rebuked, he reportedly fled the scene and the priests witnessed the exorcist's exhausting release. The children were then taken to a sacred bath, where they were baptized, and thus cleansed of any stain. They emerged from the waters of cleansing to a new life. Then they were given white robes to cover their nakedness, a symbol of the purity they gained from renouncing the devil. These robes would have been made of the same material as the sheet that covered the naked boy who was with Jesus in the garden of Gethsemane when he was arrested.

After this ceremony, the boys were returned to the priests involved in their initiation, in order to purge themselves of any violent memories of the "fires of temptation." The priests then repeated their instructions that the details of their initiation were to remain a mystery; telling others about their experiences was a sin; the boys were reminded that Hell awaits those who are disobedient. Finally, they were given food.

To a Christian priest living in the earliest years of the Church, salvation was not a joke. Priests taught that children allowed to go on living as pagans would be sent to Hell for eternity. Initiating them into "The Way" would ultimately save their souls from an eternity of pain and suffering. This must be the reason that priests took such drastic measures to save the youth of the world; the pains of the fires of sexual temptation were far less horrific than an eternity in the underworld.

Whether or not modern Catholic priests are following the tradition of institutional rape created by the earliest Christian clergy has so far eluded the public. Even a cursory look at the earliest writings of the Christians reveals that ritual rape was an institutional standard used in processing initiates. It is not unreasonable to assume that the theological justification for sodomizing young boys is still present in the ranks of Catholic priests.

GREEK THEATER

The rape of children in the modern Christian Church may not be as organized as it was when the Church first developed, but child abuse clearly remains an institutional problem. For reasons that continue to elude investigators, the Church actively fosters and protects the practice of child molestation and sexual assault. Priests have sexually abused children for centuries, and bishops have always protected these rapists from prosecution. The Catholic Church has remained very much the same for two thousand years. The problem of child rape may never be rooted out of the Church, because it is integral to the very foundations of Christianity.

Epilogue

Two hundred kids stabbed St. Cassian to death, after the Roman authorities stripped him naked, tied his hands behind his back, and handed him over to his own students. They didn't use daggers; they killed him with the thin, needle-like Roman stylus, an iron tool once used by schoolchildren to practice writing by making impressions on wax tablets. Cassian, a Christian, wasn't martyred in the Colosseum in some sort of bloody spectacle; he was poked to death by a crowd of furious boys, the youngest of whom frantically scratched furrows into his skin, lacking the strength to pierce it.

The Roman magistrate who handed Cassian over to his own charges deemed his punishment an apt reward for incredibly abusive behavior. The Romans bound him and removed his clothes, in the same manner as Cassian was accustomed to treat his own students. In good Roman judicial fashion, they hoisted him on his own petard.

SEBASTIAN, DURER

Early Christian writers fail to provide even a plausible explanation for the vehement wrath of Cassian's students, but it is clear from our texts that the boys believed their teacher got exactly what he deserved.

The students began by smashing their box-wood tablets across Cassian's face and head. According to one author, Prudentius in *Crowns of Martyrdom*, the wax-covered tablets split with a loud, audible crack before splintering into many blood-covered pieces. Next the boys proceeded to scratch and perforate his skin with their writing implements—the older ones penetrating all the way to his organs.

As the schoolchildren became fatigued by their rigorous punishment of Cassian, the soon-to-be martyr simultaneously mocked their insufficient stamina and encouraged them to finish the job with the vigor of more adult years. The boys returned his taunting by making sport of him as he bled to death; like the magistrate who labeled Cassian an abuser—or physical violator of children—the students maintained that such a drastic punishment was just.

After Cassian died, the Church declared him a martyr. Christians like Prudentius, whose short work on the death of Cassian is one of our only surviving accounts, venerated him as one of the many Christian saints who suffered the wrath of pagans for the sake of his faith. However, his death at the hands of such young, distressed children leaves students of history with several compelling questions.

Unanswered Questions

For example, why were child abusers prosecuted by pagans but dutifully protected by the early Church? Were young boys repeatedly assaulted as a result of a few rogue priests, or was physical abuse an institutional product of Christianity? And why did the pagan world respond universally with such visceral disgust for the behavior and alleged misconduct of Christians, be they priests, monks or bishops? After all, the Romans were strict disciplinarians, whose dislike for the Christians focused upon their odd sexual acts and not their inclination for rigorous training.

It would be easy, even comfortable, for people today—accustomed to a less avowedly political and more moderate form of Christianity—to imagine that the sexual practices of the early Church discussed in this book were some sort of aberration, perhaps a minor offshoot of mainstream Christian teachings. But this is not so—these avowedly sexual approaches to salvation were the mainstream of Christianity and are a firmly established part of its foundation. The notion of a sexualized Jesus may make modern worshippers cringe, but the most prominent early Church fathers did not shrink from the concept. They embraced it fully and made it the basis of many of their writings.

For example, Origen, head of the catechetical school in Alexandria, wrote a commentary on *Song of Songs*. In the introduction to this work he discusses the Christian transformation of sexual desire from that of a man for a woman—or harlot—to that of a man for Jesus. Origen makes it clear that Jesus takes the place of the woman in an explicitly sexual context. The shift from "lust" to "love of Jesus" takes place at the age of sexual maturation, under the guidance of the Church: "For everyone who comes to what they call the age of puberty loves something, whether less than rightly when he loves what he should not [which Origen has previously said is a woman or harlot], or rightly and beneficially when he loves what he should [which is Jesus, as sexual love]," writes Origen in his *Commentary on the Song of Songs*.

Origen even claims that Ignatius said Jesus was his "love crucified," using the same expression the Greeks used to express erotic love. The expression is translated as "loving affection" and is used by Origen to talk about the job of the Holy Spirit—which the exorcists were reportedly using to apply the "fires of temptation" to the prepubertal, naked, blindfolded, oiled boys. Origen says: "Thus this Paraclete, the Spirit of truth, who proceeds from the Father, goes about seeking if He may find any worthy and fit souls to whom he may reveal the excellence of that loving affection [sexual congress] which is from God."

Only "fit" boys were found capable of transforming their sexual desire, or as Origen says in one place about the bride of Solomon, that she was "now able to receive manly power and perfect mystery."

The catechetical school of Alexandria was reportedly founded by Mark. And of course Mark is the very gospel writer who, in 14:51-52, reported the presence of the naked teenage boy with Jesus in the garden of Gethsemane. In addition, according to Clement, who was also associated with the catechetical school in Alexandria, the pre-redacted version of Mark talks about Jesus' affair with yet another young man.

Jesus' Sexuality

All of these texts reveal something about the intense interest of the early Christians in the sexuality of Jesus. But of all the Christian writings dealing with the sexualization of Jesus and the role of sexuality in the Church, the most compelling is a passage by Minucius Felix, a Christian of the early third century who reported in his Octavius that the pagan world believed the early Christians ritually venerated the genitalia of their founder. Felix, taking on the role of a non-Christian, also says, "Details of the initiation of neophytes are as revolting as they are notorious."

Pedophile priests are not the inevitable and unfortunate reality of an organization that promotes the celibacy of its leadership. The rape of children is not an historical coincidence or an unfortunate circumstance perpetuated by the Catholic priesthood. Sexual assault is very much an integral aspect of Christianity itself. Sodomizing children has historically been an effective means of establishing authority and control.

When Christians first attacked the pagan environment in which they lived, they fought to undercut the authority of a competing culture that venerated gods like Venus and Bacchus, divinities associated with sexual impulses and ecstatic pleasure. Christian priests, in perfect conformity with the earliest followers of "The Way," broke from the long-established worship of the natural world and began to enforce a new social paradigm that flourished under a program of sexual abuse. Pedophile priests were an integral component of the early Church hierarchy. In fact, it is likely that Christianity would never have existed if it were not for the efforts of apostles, elders, monks, priests and bishops who promoted the decline of classical values in exchange for a new understanding of sex as an act of corruption and women as agents of vice.

The pagan world refused to embrace Christianity because it considered the fledgling cult to be adversarial to Nature itself; pagans believed Christians supported a view of the world that ran contrary to the dictates of reason. In a world that celebrated the rightful power of feminine sexual allure, the Christians taught that women were the source of all evil in the universe and that sexual intercourse was a cause of eternal damnation. From its inception, Christianity placed itself outside the traditional bounds of western culture, and institutional rape evolved as merely one means of asserting dominance, control and a change. Pedophile priests were not criminals who took refuge in the Church; they were its founders.

Dr. David C.A. Hillman earned a Ph.D. in Classics and M.S. in Bacteriology from the University of Wisconsin, where he studied the medicine and pharmacology of antiquity. *The London Times* described his research as "the last wild frontier of classical studies." Dr. Hillman's work, while firmly grounded in primary sources—the original documents of Church authorities and others—is highly controversial. It is research that many modern Church officials do not want known. His dissertation committee refused to pass him unless he removed material about the use of psychedelic drugs in antiquity; he later published the forbidden material in *The Chemical Muse*. The revelations in *Original Sin* are even more shocking, especially in light of the worldwide scandals involving pedophile Catholic priests and the higher Church authorities who have protected them and allowed child abuse to continue for years. As soon as the topic of *Original Sin* became known, Dr. Hillman's livelihood was threatened and he was told he would be blacklisted in his field of teaching. He nevertheless decided to let the truth be known and completed *Original Sin* under a threat to his ability to support himself and his children. For more information about Dr. Hillman's work, visit his home at Ronin: roninpub.com/orisin.html <http://roninpub.com/orisin.html>

www.ingramcontent.com/pod-product-compliance
Lightning Source LLC
Jackson TN
JSHW020021141224
75386JS00025B/634

* 9 7 8 1 5 7 9 5 1 1 4 4 9 *